PAINTED WOOD PROJECTS in the
Pennsylvania Folk Art Style

Alan & Gill Bridgewater

STERLING PUBLISHING CO., INC.
NEW YORK

To the memory of my paternal grandmother—Marie Evans, born of Welsh parents in Allegheny City, Pennsylvania, in 1890—who died in Wales in 1963

Alan T. Bridgewater

ACKNOWLEDGMENTS

We would like to thank everyone who has helped us with this book:

- Rachael Roberts—for the loan of the special camera.
- Lesley Woodhouse—from Fowey Library—for her wonderful, amazing, cheerful, book-finding help.
- Tracy Emmison—Humbrol Paints.
- Pebeo Paints.
- Rodman Neumann—Editor—STERLING PUBLISHING COMPANY—for all his painstaking help. Alan, Gill, and Rodman—what a great team!

Library of Congress Cataloging-in-Publication Data

Bridgewater, Alan.
    Painted wood projects in the Pennsylvania folk art style / Alan & Gill Bridgewater.
        p.   cm.
    Includes index.
    ISBN 0-8069-0508-5
    1. Painting.   2. Painted woodwork.   3. Folk art, Pennsylvania Dutch.   4. Decorative arts, Pennsylvania Dutch.   5. House furnishings.   I. Bridgewater, Gill.   II. Title.
    TT385.B75   1995
    745.7'23—dc20   95-14927
                                                                                      CIP

10 9 8 7 6 5 4 3 2 1

First paperback edition published in 1996 by
Sterling Publishing Company, Inc.
387 Park Avenue South, New York, N.Y. 10016
© 1995 by Alan & Gill Bridgewater
Distributed in Canada by Sterling Publishing
% Canadian Manda Group, One Atlantic Avenue, Suite 105
Toronto, Ontario, Canada M6K 3E7
Distributed in Great Britain and Europe by Cassell PLC
Wellington House, 125 Strand, London WC2R 0BB, England
Distributed in Australia by Capricorn Link (Australia) Pty Ltd.
P.O. Box 6651, Baulkham Hills, Business Centre, NSW 2153, Australia
Printed in Hong Kong
All rights reserved

Sterling ISBN 0-8069-0508-5 Trade
                0-8069-0509-3 Paper

Contents

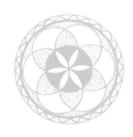

Preface

The intention of this book is to explore and demonstrate the use of all the painterly skills and techniques involved in the production of traditional Pennsylvania folk art painting.

When we saw our first Pennsylvania dower chest, we were amazed; the sheer brilliance of the colors, and the wonderful exuberant and uninhibited quality of the painted designs was *beautiful!*—it was a real eye-opener. And of course, once our eyes were opened, and we realized that Pennsylvania painting contained a treasury of pattern, motif, and color—just waiting to be unlocked—we were anxious to find the key.

But where to start? Not the least of our problems was the fact that many of the techniques used by the Pennsylvania German painters were lost. The various recipes and procedures had either been passed on by word of mouth from one generation to another or, in the rare instance, written down in books and pamphlets, the language and meanings of which are now obscure. Our objectives in exploring the Pennsylvania folk art style have included searching out lost skills, making innumerable hands-on tryouts, and then presenting our findings in a way that is easy to understand and follow.

Painted Wood Projects in the Pennsylvania Folk Art Style has been carefully shaped—with an introductory section to place the style in time and place, a section to describe specific materials and techniques, and then 20 projects. On the premise that the beginner can only really learn by doing, each project has been designed with design grids to work from and color illustrations showing each step of the painting process. This book is jam-packed with patterns, motifs, designs, painting techniques, and procedures. There are more than 40 gridded designs between the detailed projects and the extra decorative pattern examples from historical designs included in the introductory section on Pennsylvania folk art style.

Our thinking is that the beginner can work through the projects and then, having achieved a fair degree of expertise and experience, refer to the decorative pattern examples from historical designs and advance to greater things.

If you like working with brushes and paint, then what could be more stimulating and satisfying than mixing your own paints and decorating some part of your home with juicy splashes of color, rich vibrant patterns, and bold traditional Pennsylvania motifs?

A visually exciting journey into the wonderful world of American folk art decoration, an insight into Pennsylvania German painting traditions, a decorator's pattern and motif source book, a comprehensive guide to painterly techniques—*Painted Wood Projects in the Pennsylvania Folk Art Style* is all of these and then some!

Alan and Gillian Bridgewater

Pennsylvania Folk Art Style

IN 1681, WILLIAM PENN, an English Quaker, was granted a charter from King Charles II to colonize the New World area that we now know as Pennsylvania. Penn and other Quakers who had suffered religious persecution in England were seeking a land where they could freely practise their faith. In keeping with his belief that religious freedom was a natural right, Penn sent out petitions and pamphlets inviting other persecuted groups to join him in his venture.

Swedish and Finnish settlers were already well established prior to Penn's arrival. Immigrants from all over Europe were attracted to the colony as a result of Penn's liberal and tolerant beliefs and the subsequent codes and laws guaranteeing religious freedom. The colony welcomed immigrants from Germany, Switzerland, France, Holland, Sweden, Wales, Ireland, Scotland, and many other countries and regions.

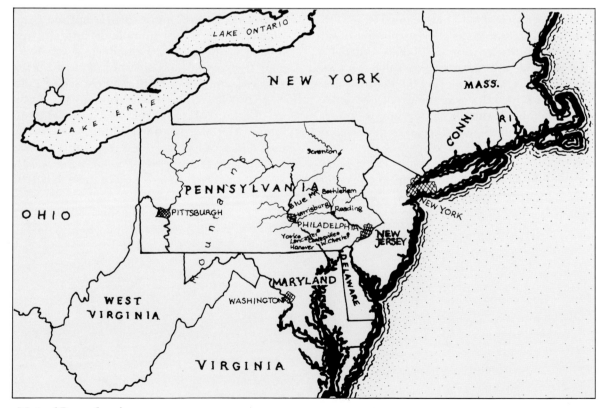

Map of Pennsylvania

HISTORY

In the context of *Painted Wood Projects in the Pennsylvania Folk Art Style,* German-speaking settlers are of paramount importance in that they came over not as individuals, but as large, tightly knit groups, sects, and congregations. It is on record that, in some instances, one-quarter of the population of certain German villages—mostly young men and women with families—decided to move as a unit to the New World. So, for example, there were the Amish, the Dunkers, the Mennonites, the Moravians, and the Schwenkfelders—all relatively large, well-organized groups.

These groups of immigrants became known as the Pennsylvania Dutch—a corruption of *Deutsch*. They settled primarily in the rich farmland counties of Northampton, Lancaster, and Berks. By the end of the colonial period, the German settlers numbered about 100,000—more than a third of the total population of Pennsylvania.

What sets the Pennsylvania German communities apart is that, from the very beginning, their aspirations diverged from English-speaking groups. The Germans showed little interest in becoming New Americans—that is to say, entering the mainstream English cultural group—but rather they set their sights on becoming independent family farmers and landowners. To a greater or lesser degree, the German settlers resisted New World assimilation in that they tended to prefer Old World German customs, beliefs, traditions, and patterns of behavior.

This assertion of their ethnic heritage, plus increasing wealth, manifested itself, perhaps more than anything else, in remembrance and application of the traditional craft of painted decorative folk art. This is not to say that the eighteenth- and nineteenth-century German settlers were alone in having a tradition of decorative painting—in fact, just about every region in Europe had such a tradition—but rather it is to say that the Pennsylvania Germans were distinctive in continuing their tradition of painting and decorating well after most European immigrants had moved on to other things.

Even more exciting—and this, we feel, is the key to the whole Pennsylvania folk art phenomenon—is that while the original decorative painting traditions died out in the Old World, the Pennsylvania Germans perpetuated their painting tradition so that it not only flourished but evolved. By the time decorative painting had travelled from the Old World to the New, been preserved in the inward-looking Pennsylvania German communities, been passed on to third- or fourth-generation Americans—with necessary adaptations to available materials and the evolution of techniques and usages—the tradition had become, as it were, dynamically revitalized. The painting was still recognizably German in origin, but it had grown and developed in a distinctively American way.

Whereas in Germany such and such a motif, design, or pattern was intended as an imitation of carving or was inspired by Gothic windows—or had drawn its inspiration from old and prestigious furniture or been used as a religious symbol—or whatever, the same motifs, patterns, and designs, remembered by New World Pennsylvania painters and decorators, were transposed and shaped by time and new conditions to become original, exciting forms of painterly decoration in their own right.

Although much of the painted decoration has its origin and meaning in ancient pagan and Christian traditions, by the time it had passed through the New World experience, its usage had more to do with pride, cultural identity, and the need to be seen as prosperous than with any ancient symbolic significance.

FOLKLORE AND MISCONCEPTIONS

If we are to fully understand and enjoy Pennsylvania German painting, it is important that we clear up a few popular misconceptions.

First, when we go to museums and see Pennsylvania German exhibits and room arrangements, it's very easy to get the impression that everything was painted and decorated. This was not the case! Okay, a great deal of it *was* painted, and, yes, the Pennsylvania German decorators did paint all manner of small mundane objects, but the everything-was-painted idea has more to do with the museums' desire to collect vivid, exciting examples than with anything else. The simple truth is that many objects were left unadorned.

Second, although popular literature and movies tend to portray Pennsylvania settlers coming home after a hard day's slog, plunking down in front of the fire, and setting to work whittling and painting—this was not the case. Yes, of course there were talented home workers, and certainly some items were painted by members of the family, but to a great extent the painting was done by full-time itinerant painters.

Third, there is a common misconception that the Pennsylvania German painters only used homemade paints—earth colors, milk paints, and such. Certainly the early painters had no choice but to use colors made from the native red clay and other homemade mixes, but, then again, as soon as factory- or shop-made pigments became freely available, those were used. That said, since the factory-made products were only available as basic ingredients—powder pigments, oils, mineral spirits, and such—then to that extent the painters still had to mix their paints.

A fourth point is that while Pennsylvania painting was rooted in the German immigrants' desire to stay true to a remembered tradition of patterns, colors, and techniques of working, local variations and changes were inevitable. Aside from the effects of local materials and the vagaries of memory, these traditions were passed from one generation to the next with the natural tendency of the younger generation to want to outdo the older. In simplistic terms, with the passage of time, designs got bigger and sharper, colors brighter, patterns more stylized, and so on.

AMISH AND FRAKTUR

One only has to visit a museum exhibit of Pennsylvania folk art to see that a great deal of the painted imagery on chests, benches, and the like draws its inspiration directly from fraktur—the art of decorative manuscript illustration. For example, many of the unicorns, tulips, hex-stars, and angels—as painted on dower chests—appear to be direct copies of earlier fraktur illustrations.

Of all the German religious sects who first immigrated to Pennsylvania, and who decorated their furniture, the Amish are, perhaps, at one and the same time the most important and the most enigmatic. We say this because, although they are in our day the most visible—they are relatively prosperous, the men still wear long black coats and black hats, the women wear bonnets, and they all shun automobiles—they are also very private.

Although the Old Order Amish—a subgroup of Mennonites who now number about 18,000—are only a small minority within Pennsylvania, they are of particular importance in the context of Pennsylvania fraktur and consequently in the context of painted decoration in that their philosophy incorporates a resistance to change. Striving to live essentially in the past, their homes are sparsely furnished, and, of course, they have held on to their decorative traditions longer than other immigrant groups who adapted freely to changing times. This being the case, Pennsylvania German Amish painted objects, furniture, and fraktur manuscripts—in museums and in their homes—offer insights into the decorative ideas and techniques used in both the recent past and the distant past.

MOTIFS AND SYMBOLISM

The Amish practised fraktur manuscript illustration until the late nineteenth century, during which time their imagery, colors, and symbols were instilled with meaning. To know more about Pennsylvania folk art decoration, we need to look at Amish fraktur designs and their symbolism.

Birds

A great many pieces of painted furniture feature various standing, flying, and perched birds. Birds are thought to symbolize joy, delight, and the human soul, with pairs of doves being the symbol for love and marriage.

Pennsylvania fraktur. A baptismal or birth certificate (taufschein) *by C. M., Lancaster County, 1796. We have left out the lettering that occurs within the heart shape. Note the characteristic motifs—heart, birds, angel, stylized tulips, and the entwined vine.*

Pennsylvania dower chest, Lancaster County, 1764. H 24¼" × W 48¾" × D 22¼". An early painted chest, the architectural details are made from white oak pinned/pegged on the tulip wood chest. (Winterthur Museum, Wilmington, DE)

Dower Chest

Traditionally every Pennsylvania German maiden was given a hope, or "dower," chest. The idea springs from the ancient custom of the woman giving the husband a gift and/or a man presenting a gift, often of his own making, to his bride or her parents. That said, the Amish had/have a tradition of giving their children sets of "starter" furniture, with both sexes getting a large chest.

All this means that not all of the painted chests were "dower" chests—some were specifically made for the male children of the family. Although the chests were typically built from inexpensive, rough slab wood like pine, the paints and the labor were expensive. The chests were valued both symbolically and monetarily, so that they were preserved as treasured possessions.

The symbols on the chests are, in most cases, direct copies from fraktur greeting cards, baptismal certificates, and such. In broad general terms, the dower chest painters favored unicorns, tulips, vase/pots with lug handles, stylized hearts, snakes, birds, crowned figures, fraktur dates, names, and initials, with the whole design being more or less symmetrical.

Hearts

The heart symbol has its beginnings in France in the twelfth century when the human heart was thought to be the seat of emotion and love. In that context, the greatest thing that a lover could offer his beloved—his "sweetheart"—was his heart. In the late Middle Ages, the heart symbol was given a Christian significance, when the heart motif was portrayed in art and literature as being the "Heart of Our Lord." From about the sixteenth century, the heart found new meaning as a romantic motif.

In Pennsylvania, the German-speaking immigrants used the heart motif on just about everything from iron work, embroidery, woodcarving, and biscuit cutters to frakturs, pottery, and, of course, painted furniture.

Detail from the front panel of a "Unicorn" dower chest, 1803, Berks County. Note the use of characteristic motifs and patterns—tulips, a crowned figure, zigzags, and lines and dots.

Mermaid

The mermaid motif has to do with an ancient, pagan German belief that a half-woman, half-fish creature could give protection from the evil eye. In Germany, the mermaid motif is seen in carvings on doorways, in embroideries, and in gingerbread moulds. In eighteenth-century Bavaria the motif was used on lodging-house and inn signs.

The painted mermaid seen on Pennsylvania chests was most likely considered a symbol of good luck.

Star-Circles

The star-circle, often referred to as the hex sign, found painted on chests and barns and on just about everything else in between, was thought of as being powerful protection against evil spirits. That said, the star-circle design was a motif that was traditionally used on all the household utensils that were gifted to the bride. In Germany typically it was carved, whereas in Pennsylvania it was painted.

In Germany, the six-pointed, compass-formed star associated with marriages was found carved on the bride's chair, bed-warmers, pastry boards, and such. Some experts consider the design to be a sun symbol.

Another form of compass-drawn star is the "Basque Cross." This motif, looking a bit like four commas whirling around in a circle, was traditionally found on tombstones.

Pennsylvania barn with painted hex decoration, possibly by Noah Weiss, from an 1862 photograph, Steinsberg, Lehigh County.

Fraktur/drawing, 1800, Southeast Pennsylvania. Note the traditional motifs—the stylized tulips, the vase with lug/jug ears, and the symmetrical layout.

Tulips

Of all the motifs used by the painters, the tulip has been one of the most popular. In the early sixteenth century tulip flowers were introduced into Europe— into the Low Countries—from Constantinople. By about 1637, they were so popular that they became the subject of an amazing speculation that we now term "tulipomania." At the height of this craze, single bulbs were sold for extraordinary prices and fortunes were made and lost. The cult of the tulip swept across Holland, Germany, and the rest of Europe, where the easily drawn tulip design became a decorative motif on just about everything from woodcarving and embroidery to silverwork and, of course, painted furniture.

Pennsylvania German fraktur manuscripts—baptismal certificates, greeting cards, book plates, and the like—are jam-packed with tulip motifs. We think it fair to suppose that, while the immigrants didn't get to bring much furniture, most of them would have had Bibles and various personal documents. What better than to copy fraktur designs—expecially tulips!

Although various experts consider that the tulip symbolized the Holy lily, with the three petals standing for the Trinity, we feel that, more than anything else, the tulip was used simply because it reminded the Germans of their homeland.

A painted candle box, 1800—with strawberry, grape, and vine imagery. Painted in traditional colors—yellow, red, and leaf-green.

Unicorn

The unicorn, as found painted on fraktur manuscripts, dower chests, and various other items of furniture, was regarded as the symbol of virtue, holy and virginal purity. That said, European heraldry is full of horses, lions, and mythical beasts. If we were to place certain pieces of European carving side by side with examples of Pennsylvania painted chests and frakturs, it would be clear that there is a strong connection between the three, with the unicorn being used, perhaps more than anything else, as a heraldic symbol.

One expert suggests that both the horse and the unicorn motifs, as seen on dower chests, were intended to convey the message to young girls that true love, Holy love—like the horse or unicorn—can only be captured by a virgin. Or, to put it another way, the painted unicorns on the chests were a quite intentional, constant visual reminder to behave!

Zigzag

The zigzag border pattern, as seen on all manner of painted Pennsylvania items, has its roots in Swiss and German woodcarving. Traditionally, zigzag patterns were found on just about everything that could be carved—boxes, dairy equipment, laundry boards, cooking items, and all manner of other household objects. We wonder whether the zigzag might almost be thought of as archetypal in that it is one of the first patterns made by children.

Detail from Pennsylvania tin tray, painted in traditional colors. Attributed to Frederick Zeitz, Philadelphia, 1874.

COLORS

The Pennsylvania painters used specific colors for a variety of reasons that encompassed availability and tradition. On the one hand, the early painters had no choice but to use subdued colors like red and yellow made from local clays and various browns made from nut and root juices, but, on the other hand, their choice of color was, in part, governed by traditional design usage. So, for example, since red and yellow were traditionally associated with marriage and family, they were used on dower chests and small household items. And then again, they favored black outlines and red and yellow details on a green ground.

Even when a full range of colors was available commercially, the painters still stayed with a relatively limited range—those that they were familiar with.

In brief—and keeping in mind that there are always exceptions to the rule—the Pennsylvania folk palette is made up of vermilion, chrome-yellow, yellow ochre, dark leaf green, light leaf green, Prussian blue, blue-grey, burnt umber, black, and white. If you have any doubts about whether a shade is appropriate, a reliable rule is to avoid pastel and Day-Glo colors, and go for the basic primaries—red, yellow, blue, black, and white—all muddied slightly with a small amount of raw umber.

DECORATIVE PATTERN EXAMPLES FROM HISTORICAL DESIGNS

Pennsylvania folk art style is displayed in a wide range of forms—from hex signs and frakturs to dower chests and other household items. Here we offer a directory of gridded patterns taken from historical examples that you may use to create your own additional projects or to expand on the twenty projects that we present in detail.

Two hex designs—worked with a pair of compasses and a straightedge.

Fraktur design from a birth and baptismal certificate, Pennsylvania, 1826—ink and watercolor.

Detail from a 1720 dower chest—stencilled and painted. Note the characteristic motifs of tulips, hex-flower, zigzags, pillar, and arch.

Detail from a dower chest panel, Berk County, 1778. A symmetrical design with tulips, a lug-eared vase, comma-shaped flowers, a crown-like flower, zigzags, and vines, all set in an arched panel.

Fraktur paper-cut love letter. Christian Strenge, Lancaster County, 1800. Hand-drawn and cut out—the lettering occurs within the heart shapes and in the middle.

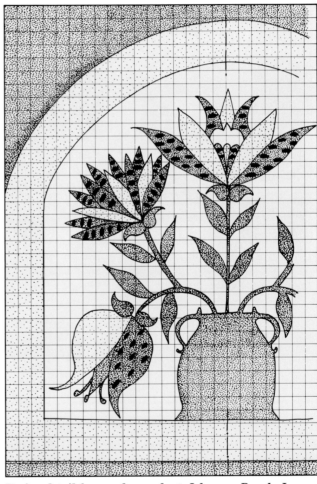

(Top) This Pennsylvania design almost certainly draws its inspiration from an earlier English inlay. (Bottom) Design by Christian Selzer, eighteenth century, Dauphin County.

Design detail from a dower chest. Johannes Ranck, Jonestown, Lebanon County, 1790.

Dower chest side panel. Lancaster County, 1780.

Brush-stroke painting. (Top) Repeat design from a bucket, on a dark ground. 1825. (Bottom) Motif from a coffee pot, on a dark ground. Date unknown.

(Left) Border design from a music book cover, drawn and painted, Bucks County, 1813. (Right) Border design from a fraktur taufschein (baptismal certificate). John Hetzel, Lancaster County, 1789.

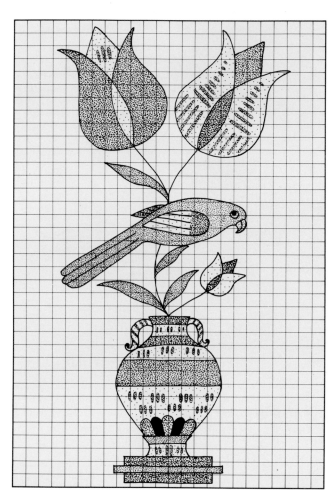

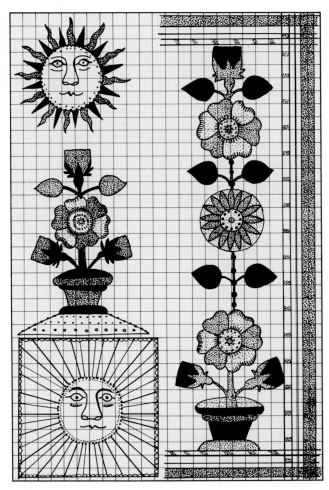

Fraktur detail from a baptismal certificate. John Valentin Schuller, Northumberland County, 1810. Although the motif is in itself unsymmetrical, the pattern is reversed for the other half of the fraktur to make a symmetrical design.

Fraktur border design from a baptismal certificate, drawn and painted. Henry Dutge, Berks County, 1784.

Brush-stroke painting. (Top) Design painted on a coffee pot. James Fulivier, 1825. (Bottom) Design on a tray—stencilled, in part—1825.

(Top left) Detail from a fireboard, early nineteenth century. (Top right) Male figure from a dower chest panel, Lancaster County, 1780. (Middle) Mermaid detail from a dower chest, 1790. (Bottom) Detail from a chest of drawers.

Detail from a dower chest, circa 1775–1800—with characteristic motifs of tree of life, Adam and Eve, the snake, hex flowers, birds, stylized tulips, and vines.

17

Basic Materials and Techniques

I F YOU ARE going to decorate a wall, door, chest, or some other found item in the spirit of the American Pennsylvania tradition, then, more than anything else, you need to be "at one" with your paints. You need to be able to confidently predict how the paints relate and react one with another, how such and such a paint type behaves when it has been over-varnished, how long the selected paint is going to take to dry, how the colors appear when dry, and so on. In the context of Pennsylvania folk art style painting, knowledge and understanding go hand in hand with freedom of technique and pleasure of execution.

Although the Pennsylvania painters—the family members and itinerant painters of the seventeenth, eighteenth, and nineteenth century—were limited by and large to using a relatively small number of homemade paint recipes to decorate their handmade furniture and their pioneer home interiors, we advocate using a combination of homemade and modern shop-bought paints to decorate both new and old found items. Keeping this in mind, it is also important that you know what happens when you lay new paint over old.

PAINTS

As we see it, the secret of painting and decorating in the Pennsylvania tradition today is to limit yourself to using a few basic paint and varnish types—water-based and oil, flat, glossy, and transparent—and to restrict yourself to using a relatively small palette of authentic colors. It doesn't matter too much if you use shop bought paints as long as you stay within the traditional color range.

Part of the fun and excitement of painting in the Pennsylvania folk art style is that the tradition allows, and even encourages, a great deal of trial-and-error experimentation. If you look closely at museum originals—dower chests, chairs, boxes, and the like—it's plain to see that in the normal course of events the folk artists were more than happy to chop and change the designs, to paint over mistakes, and generally to explore new design themes.

More than anything else, painting in the Pennsylvania folk art style is about enjoyment—the pure, naive, tactile, almost child-like pleasure of working with color and paint.

Flat Paint

Flat paint has the appearance when dry of being perfectly flat, or matt, and chalky in texture. Basically there are two flat paint types; there are the oil-based undercoats and alkyds that need to be thinned with white mineral spirit, and there are the water-based emulsions, vinyls, latexes, distempers, and buttermilks that need to be thinned with water.

As to your choice of flat paint, much depends on what it is that you want to decorate and, of course, the availability of the materials. We tend to favor shop-bought matt vinyl/latex PVA (polyvinyl-acetate) type paints and homemade milk paint for the plain and simple reason that water-based paints are so wonderfully user-friendly. They are easy to mix, the brushes can be washed under running water, the colors can be modified easily, the paint is work-dry in a relatively short time, and, perhaps most important of all, the flat, slightly sheeny finish looks authentic.

Flat paint can be used on wood as an undercoat for gloss paint, on plaster as a finish, on floors, and so on. Depending on the type of flat paint and where it is to be used, it might need to be protected with varnish and/or wax polish. If you are painting a ceiling, you simply apply the paint and the job is done. But then again, if you are decorating a chest, the flat paint needs to be protected with a coat of varnish and a burnishing of wax polish. That acknowledged, some modern flat paints don't take kindly to being varnished. If you have any doubts about the mixability of your selected paint and varnish, it's best to have a try-out on a small corner and see what happens.

Milk Paints

Traditionally, the Pennsylvania painters favored milk paints, sometimes known as buttermilk colors. Old accounts describe milk paint as being made from fresh milk colored with such agents as fruit juice, blood, soot, clay, crushed brick, tree bark, and mustard.

We have experimented with various mixes, and, to date, the recipe that works best for us is one made up from instant, nonfat dried milk powder and powdered earth color pigments and/or model-makers' acrylic color.

This method is wonderfully easy and direct; all we do is add water to the milk powder—to make a thick, creamy mix—and then stir in the colors to suit. The opacity can be modified by adding more or less water, and the density of the color can be adjusted by adding more or less pigment.

Just in case you think that milk paints are a crazy idea in this modern, centrally heated, sophisticated world of ours, they do not smell nor do they wash off—and they do not remain sticky. A milk-paint finish is characterized by being flat and clear—much like a shop-bought latex paint—with the added advantage that the finish dries to a beautiful, slight misty, antique translucence.

For added protection—just in case you are worried about possible problems with hygiene, termites, or the cat and/or the children licking the paint off—you can give the milk paint a finish coat of matt sheen varnish.

Gloss Paint

Traditionally the Pennsylvania painters used both flat and glossy paints. For example, a chest might be given a flat undercoat, then painted with a gloss ground, then have the design picked out in gloss, and then finally be varnished, with all the layers being oil-based. Or then again, the chest might be first stained with a thin water-based colorwash, and then decorated with oil-based gloss paint before being finished with a thin, glossy oil-based glaze. And yet again, some decorators used oil-based paints for both the ground color and the design, and then finished off to a dull gloss by giving the piece a generous wipe-over with oil.

From one painter to another, just about every possible combination of water- and oil-based paints were used.

The main point to bear in mind when using a traditional oil-based gloss paint is that it takes considerably longer to dry than a comparable water-based paint. For example, if you were to use an old recipe that recommended a mix of linseed oil, turpentine, and pigment, then you might well have to wait for two or three *weeks* between stages.

We favor short-cutting the old techniques by using, whenever possible, water-based paint for both the ground and the decoration, and then achieving a glossy finish by giving the whole works a generous coat of high-shine varnish and/or wax sheen polish. We sometimes lay on a modern acrylic ground, use a mix of varnish and artist's oil colors for the decoration, and then finish off by using a glaze made by mixing a small amount of oil-based color with varnish.

The principal advantage of using such techniques is that it is possible to achieve a fully decorated piece with a high glossy finish in days rather than weeks.

TRANSPARENT FINISHES, STAINS, AND VARNISHES

Transparent finishes, stains, and varnishes can be either oil- or water-based.

Water-Based Stains and Colors

In the context of giving bare wood a thin coat of clear color, we favor using nothing more elaborate than watercolor. All we do is mix artist's quality powder paint, or poster color, with water, and then lay the resultant watery color on as a thin wash.

We use a full range of colors, everything from ochre, umber, and soft yellow to straight primary colors like yellow, blue, and red. The resultant finishes are bright and yet subtle, with the added attraction that the pigment bleeds into the wood without leaving a skin.

The uneven take-up of the color into the layers of hard and soft grain—as found in a good many softwoods—results in an especially beautiful, rippled old-and-much-worn effect.

The only real disadvantage of using a watercolor stain is that the water lifts the wood grain. This being

so, once the wash is dry, the wood needs to be given a quick sanding with a fine-grade sandpaper to remove the whiskers and nibs of grain.

Glazes and Washes

Glazes and washes are no more or less than a thin, semi-transparent film of oil- or water-based color. Although, strictly speaking, a wash is water-based and a glaze oil-based, it's worth bearing in mind that many books, old and new, confuse the terms.

The only real differences between a wash and a glaze—apart from the mix—are the application and context. Broadly speaking—and keeping in mind that there are always exceptions to the rule—a water-based wash is applied directly onto bare wood and/or onto a flat, matt paint, whereas an oil-based glaze can be used on just about any dry surface. Keeping that in mind, if you want to lay a water-based wash on a shiny surface, such as varnish or oil paint, then either you have to mix a few drops of dishwashing liquid into the wash, or you have to wipe the surface over with a clean, soapy cloth. If you miss out on the soap, the chances are that the wash will "crawl" and run off.

An old, much-worn effect can be achieved either by using a glaze made from varnish and artist's oil color thinned down with turps or by using a thin wash.

If you have doubts about the durability of a finish, then consider protecting it with either matt varnish or beeswax polish.

Varnish Stain

Old-time Pennsylvania painters were very fond of using varnish stains. Of all the varnish-type stains and

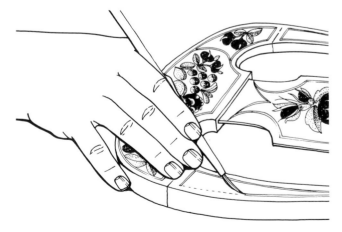

Striping or lining brush—used for painting long, fine lines.

glazes on the market—and these are many and varied—in our experience nothing really betters a simple homemade mix of artist's oil color paint and clear varnish. For us, such a mix is a high scorer in that it is easy to make, the color range possibilities are endless, the density is variable, and it is swift, inexpensive, and easy to apply. If you want a thinner mix—one that will readily bleed into the wood—all you do is add mineral/white spirit to the basic mix.

The only real disadvantage of using varnish stain is that it is all too easy to lay on an overly thick coat, in which case the finish tends to appear too bright and treacly.

BRUSHES

Brushes come in a great many shapes and sizes; there are draggers, grainers, stipplers, Japanese calligraphy brushes, and so on—the list is confusing and seemingly endless.

Generally, we tend to use four brush types. These are the ordinary, home decorator's brush, as might be purchased from just about any general hardware supplier, the long-haired brush, as used by oil and watercolor artists, the Japanese calligraphy brush, and the flat, soft-haired brush, as used for laying on watercolor washes.

In the ordinary course of events, we might lay on a coat of flat paint with a decorator's brush, block in a panel of ground color with a wide, flat, soft-haired wash brush, pick put the designs with a fine-point artist's brush—round or long sable—use a Japanese brush for painting leaves and petals, and then give the whole works a coat of varnish with another decorator's brush.

The size of the brush will, of course, depend on the object being painted and your selected paints. We favor using brushes that are about ½″ to 1½″ wide for laying on large areas of color and small-size sables for painting the design details. Small brushes, as used by artists, are numbered according to size—the lower the number, the smaller the brush. If you are a beginner, it is best to start by getting three good-quality sable brushes—small, medium, and big—and then to buy intermediate sizes when you know from experience what the brushes can do.

Japanese brushes are special in that they are capable of producing a seemingly infinite variety of strokes. The shape of the head, with its beautiful flexible tip,

Japanese calligraphy brush—used for brush-stroke work. The heads are particularly sensitive and expressive.

allows for super-sensitive control. By simply applying more or less pressure, it is possible to increase or decrease the thickness of the line. By loading the brush with paint and wiping the brush down-and-off in a single continuous stroke, the brush produces a characteristic leaf shape. If you enjoy using quality tools, then you might prefer using Japanese brushes for all the small detail work.

Fine-point sable brushes, as used by watercolor artists, are particularly useful for painting in delicate details. The heads are fine but firm.

Care and Cleaning of Brushes

Being mindful that to a great extent brushes improve with age, it pays to look after them. When you get a new brush—the large type used for laying on broad areas of ground color and for varnishing—first give it a good rap to knock out loose bristles, and then wash it in warm water.

Old-time painters traditionally gave new brushes "a good start" by using them first for laying on undercoats and ground colors. The procedure removed most of the loose hairs, and "knocked" the brush head to shape. Their thinking was that loose bristles can more easily be picked off an undercoat than off a must-be-perfect top coat.

As to cleaning brushes, those used for water-based paint—powders and acrylics—can be easily washed under running water. Oil paintbrushes—meaning those used for oil-based paints and varnishes—have to be cleaned with mineral/white spirit. We usually wipe as much paint as possible off on newspaper, dab the brush around in a jar of spirit to remove the bulk of the oil paint or varnish from between the bristles, repeat the procedure in a jar of liquid soap, and then follow up by wiping it on a bar of hard soap and washing the brush under running water.

Once the brushes are clean, shake off the loose water, shape the heads by wrapping them in paper or foil, and put them to one side to dry.

Our main rules of thumb for brush care are—

• Never leave a paint-covered brush for later—you will be sure to forget it, and regret it.
• Never drop a brush in a jar of spirit or water and expect it to clean itself.
• Never leave brushes—dirty or clean—standing on their heads.

PREPARING THE SURFACE TO BE DECORATED

First and foremost, it's important to state categorically that you must on no account start painting your "great-granny's" three-hundred-year-old chest. If the chest is no more or less than a plain pine box, or a common or garden piece of 1950s white wood, or a flea market find, then, no problem; go ahead. But if your found piece could possibly be at all old, or there is any suggestion that there might be interesting designs or images under the top coat, or it is in any way unusual, then have it checked out by an expert.

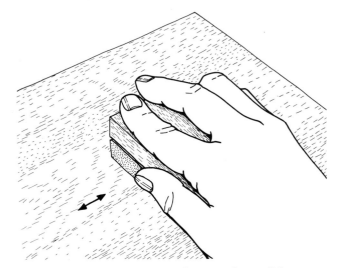

Sanding block—made from cork or wood—used for supporting sandpaper when sanding large, flat smooth surfaces. Always try to sand in the direction of the grain.

Before a surface can be painted—whether a door, a piece of furniture, or some other household item—all the fittings need to be carefully removed, nails and screws need to be extracted, cracks and holes need to be filled, and the surface needs to be sanded.

We usually work through the stages as follows—

• Keeping in mind that flea market finds sometimes turn out to be priceless antiques, we make sure that our selected piece is not, in fact, a valuable collector's item.
• When we are going to decorate a worn and battered piece, we start by deciding how much of the original wear-and-tear texture needs to be saved. For example, a curious knothole, old brass screws, a hole made good with a brass plate, or whatever are all potentially features that might well add to the overall image and feel of the piece.
• Having decided what needs to be saved, we then make a judgment as to how much of the original paint needs to be removed. We say this because, in many instances, old pitted and dented paint has an innate beauty that only adds to the overall texture. If you look at old Pennsylvania chests and the like, it's plain to see that the two hundred or so years of paint, chips, kicks, dirt, dust, spills, knocks, stains, mends, and repainting have all contributed to what is an irreplaceable patina. This being the case, if you are planning to paint an old piece, you should not necessarily be trying to clean it down to bare wood.

• Once we have made a judgment as to how much of the original finish needs to be saved, we take our selected paints and varnishes, and we have a small try-out on part of the piece that is going to remain hidden from view. So, for example, we might turn the box over to reveal a painted base or edge and make a few paint strokes. If the paint stays put and doesn't stain, lift, or bubble, for instance, then our way is clear to proceed.

• When we have checked everything over and repaired needy areas with a plaster filler and/or new wood insets, we then sand the piece with a fine-grade sandpaper or steel wool.

• When we have achieved what we consider is a desirable finish, we then start painting.

• Finally, once we have decorated the piece with one or other of the techniques, we screw any fixtures back in place, and date and sign the base.

SIZING AND TRANSFERRING THE DESIGN

Once you have chosen a suitable piece to be decorated—it might be anything from a chest or chair, to a door, wall, or box—and after you have made decisions as to the design, then comes the tricky task of drawing the design to size, making tracings, and transferring the design to the piece. If you are simply going for an all-over paint texture, like marbling or graining, then there is no transferring process. But, if you want to set out a specific design, then this stage is critical.

Let's say, then, that you have a large chest that you want to embellish with a traditional three-panel motif. We recommend that you start by looking at our designs and at any other illustrations such as photographs that you have at hand. Once you have a clear understanding of how the panel designs relate to our chest, then consider them in relation to the specific chest you have chosen for decoration. For example, when we came to design our three-panel horse-and-unicorn chest (refer to Project 18) we could see by the size of our research photograph that the spacing from left to right across the chest ran ¼" for the first side margin, ¾" for the first panel, ¼" for the left-of-center margin, 1" for the middle panel, ¼" for the right-of-center margin, ¾" for the last panel, and ¼" for the last margin. Reduced to ¼" step-offs, the proportions ran 1, 3, 1, 4, 1, 3, 1—a total of 14 units.

Once we had the proportions, we measured the length of our chest, divided that length into 14 divisions, and then enlarged the step-offs to fit. In the real measurements of our chest, a single unit became 3", three units became 9", and so on.

Enlarging

Sooner or later, you will come across a design that you want to enlarge. Let's say, for example, that you like one or other of our designs and you want to make it larger so that it fits the side of your chest. If we say something like "the scale is one grid square to ¼"," this establishes the correspondence of the gridded design to the size of the original design. All you need do is enlarge the grid and design until the grid squares measure ¼".

If the design is relatively small, you simply take this book along to a photocopy shop and get them to enlarge the design or do it yourself. Of course, there are times when we might well say something like "the scale is one grid square to 1"." In this case, the 24-square width of the grid would need to be blown up to 24". You can either take the book to a copy shop, have a same-size copy made, cut it in half, and then have each half blown up to size, or you can use the square-by-square grid construction method.

Say, for example, one of our designs states that "the scale is one grid square to 3"." This means that if the design in the book is 12 squares wide and 20 squares long, then the recommended enlarged size is 36" wide and 60" long. This being the case, you would get yourself a large sheet of paper, set it out with a 3" grid, and then painstakingly copy off the design details one square at a time.

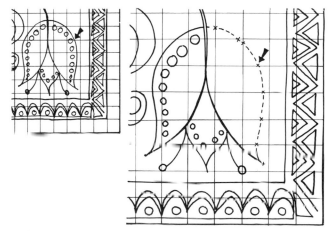

Using the grid method to enlarge a design. Map out the design by transferring the grid cross-over points, and then link them to achieve the desired line.

Although our scale and grid sizes relate to the designs of museum and collection originals, this is not to say that you can't change the design size to suit your needs. If, for example, you want to work a design quite a bit smaller, there's nothing to prevent you from making the reduction except that working some designs at a much reduced size sometimes poses technical problems. Painting the unicorns at a large chest size is one thing, but painting them at the size of a desk miniature is something again.

When you have enlarged the design—either with a photocopier, or by using the grid method—make a good, clear tracing and pin up the master design so that it is in easy view.

Transferring the Design

Once you have drawn the design at the desired size, then comes the task of transferring it onto the item/area to be decorated. Let's say, for example, that you have decided to decorate a three-panel chest, the surfaces have been prepared, and you are ready to go.

The working stages are—

• Rework the back of the tracing with a soft pencil.
• Set the tracing down on the surface to be decorated, align it with a centerline or guidelines, and fix it in place with tabs of masking tape.
• Take a hard pencil, or, better still, a ballpoint pen, and a ruler, and very carefully draw over the outer edge lines of the three panels.
• Remove the tracing and use the color of your choice to block in the three panels.
• When the paint is completely dry, reposition the tracing so that it is aligned with the painted panels, and press-transfer the lines of the design.
• Remove the tracing and paint in the large areas of color.
• When the paint is dry, replace the tracing, and reestablish any details that you have painted over.

And so you continue—repeatedly painting in areas, and transferring the details—until the design is complete.

The important thing to bear in mind when you are doing the groundwork—enlarging, transferring, and such—is that these prepainting stages set the scene for all that are to come. Okay, so the transferring may be a bit tedious, and you may not be so happy with a pencil and ruler—but just stick with it!

PAINTING—COLOR AND DESIGN

Being aware that working within the spirit of the old-time Pennsylvania painters does, by definition, involve us in a great deal of exploration and experimentation, we will by necessity be using quite a range of recipes and techniques. There are one or two golden rules that you must keep to if you are to avoid mess-ups.

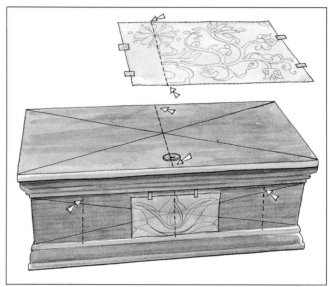

Whenever possible, draw in a centerline to help with alignment.

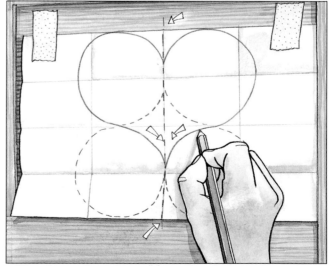

Align the tracing with the centerline, fix it in place with tabs of masking tape, and press-transfer the design with a hard pencil or ballpoint pen.

If you are laying on new paint over old, or using a homemade recipe in conjunction with modern shop-bought paints, then you must always have a pre project tryout to ensure that the paints are compatible. We once mixed a milk paint—milk powder, powder pigment, and acrylic color—brushed the mix over a chest as a ground color, let it dry, and then picked out the decoration with a shop-bought matt alkyd or vinyl paint. Everything looked fine, at first; the colors were crisp and clear, and the texture was just perfect. We stood back to admire our handiwork, and then it started to happen. The ground color suddenly began inexorably to bubble and pucker its way through the decoration to the extent that within about five minutes, all that was left was a flaky scabrous mess.

The moral of this sorry tale is that you must always check out your materials before you start painting for real. And, of course, it's no good simply brushing the tryout paints side by side; they must be set down one on top of another, and in the same order as planned for the project.

You must always let the paint dry completely between coats, especially when you are laying water- and oil-based colors one over another. For instance, if you were to lay on an oil-based base coat, and then rush straight into the decoration without first waiting for the base to dry, anything might happen. The coats might well craze and/or bleed, there might be a chemical change between coats, and so on.

We are not suggesting that you only use tried-and-tested techniques and mixes—far from it—all we are emphasizing is that you must run your "experiments" on scrap wood rather than on your selected piece.

Traditional Colors

The colors used by the Pennsylvania painters were more a product of evolution and necessity than of conscious design. That is to say, the color range was limited because the paints were typically homemade from found materials. So, for example, red earthenware clay was used to make the characteristic brick red color; yellow clay was used to make the soft ochre and yellows; the plant madder was used for making deep red; soot and candle carbon were used to make black; oak bark was used to make a range of browns; and so on. The painters simply used the products that were available—everything from earth colors and metal oxides, to plant juices and animal extracts—since, at least initially, manufactured paints were not readily available.

The color range reflected the environment in which the painters lived and worked.

Even when shop and catalogue paints were available, the painters continued to prefer the muted range of natural colors that they were used to. The most commonly used colors were a brick red, a red-brown crimson, raw-umber brown, chrome-yellow, yellow ochre, blue-green, blue, a whole range of browns, and various shades of black and white. The traditional colors are all at the soft or muted end of the range, with all of them appearing to contain, to a lesser or greater degree, a small amount of umber and/or ochre plus various impurities.

In many ways, it could be said that the impurities are responsible for the depth and character of the color. For instance, when you are able to visit a museum and have a close-up look at a chest, you may be able to see that many of the colors are flecked and speckled with small particles of black and brown, which is probably iron oxide. And then again, some of the colors would be slightly bumpy to the touch—if you were allowed to touch the piece—as if they contained particles of sand.

If you like the look and "feel" of some of these old-time colors, you might try boosting your paints by adding a sprinkling of such impurities. You could, perhaps, add a very small amount of iron filings or red sand to the basic mix.

Traditional Designs

In the one hundred and forty years between about 1680 and 1820, it is estimated that well over 70,000 German-speaking immigrants settled in Pennsylvania. As pointed out earlier, sometimes whole villages or congregations decided to emigrate from their German or Swiss homes. It was, perhaps, the size and particular makeup of the Pennsylvania German-speaking groups of settlers that made possible the continuance of their "German" identity and way of life. They tended to preserve their culture or take as their first inspiration the elements and traditions they brought with them or that they remembered.

Having said that, nevertheless we can note the contribution of many factors in their use of design and color. The color range grew and evolved out of the environment in which the Pennsylvania painters worked—their farming and living activities, their strong cultural identity, the availability of materials—and the same can be said for the designs. In many ways

Pennsylvania dower chest. 52½" wide, Lancaster County, 1780. Note all of the traditional motifs—the flowers and vase, the stylized tulips, the zigzag border design, and the figure in costume—all set within a three-panel layout.

Unicorn dower chest. Project 18, our favorite. Based on several examples from Berks County, Pennsylvania, made between 1790 and 1803.

the designs were shaped not so much by the conscious effort of the decorators, but rather by all manner of influences coming together. Everything played a part: the strength of the mother country culture, the American experience, the character of the rural American villages in which the Pennsylvania Germans worked, new ideas from imported items and illustrations, the shape, size and function of the furniture that they were being called upon to decorate, changing fashions within the community, and, of course, the tools and materials that they used. What we think of as being characteristic Pennsylvania folk art style was, to some degree, shaped by all of these elements.

When the Pennsylvania Germans settled in America—the New World—they brought with them a whole heritage of old-world traditions, customs, ornament,

and design. They didn't actually consciously "decide" to work in a particular way or tradition, they simply carried on their lives in much the same manner as they had always done. When, for example, a father gave a daughter a dower chest—and either painted the designs himself or at least paid a travelling painter to do the job for him—he wasn't setting out to do anything different; he was simply doing as his father had done before him.

Unicorns, as seen on Pennsylvania German dower chests, symbolized love, purity, and virginity. Note also the characteristic tulip, the zigzag border, and the symmetrical arrangement of the whole design.

Tulips in vase panel from a Pennsylvania dower chest.

Naturally enough, the first- and second-generation American painters favored traditional German and Swiss designs that reminded them of "the old country"—hearts, unicorns, tulips, horsemen, zigzag patterns, with fraktur manuscript writing, hex signs, and dotted highlights.

Having established that Pennsylvania painting—the colors, designs, and traditional ways of working—was initially no more than the carrying-on of old-world traditions, we agree with others who have long recognized that the most exciting Pennsylvania designs are those that were painted by third- and fourth-generation Americans. Whereas the early pioneers were perpetuating old-world styles, the new Americans were building and developing on those traditions. If, for example, we look at a whole range of Pennsylvania chests in a museum, the later ones clearly have a punchy dynamism, with the designs being bolder and the colors being brighter and fresher. Of course even later Pennsylvania folk art painted imagery leaves no doubt that it has its roots in German folk art; but that said, the feeling comes across that the Pennsylvania German artists found a new vitality and were able to blossom and develop full in the free, fertile soil of the New World in a way that they never had in their homeland.

As we touched on in the first chapter, particularly in the section on motifs and symbolism, the Pennsylvania folk art painted designs are made up from traditional German and Swiss folk art patterns, with a generous scattering of designs and motifs from other European traditions thrown in for good measure.

Hex motifs, in the form of six-pointed stars set within circles, are thought to have to do with a medieval German belief that witches on horseback—nightmares—rode through the night looking to do harm. So the story goes that the symbols, as seen painted on Pennsylvania barns, are talismanic designs used to scare away demons. Many of these circles are drawn out five or more feet in diameter.

Although we relish the "scare-away-witches" story, and certainly some European cultures do carve and paint such symbols on door lintels and such, we suspect that in the late nineteenth and early twentieth centuries the Pennsylvania painters continued the practice for no other reason than that they simply enjoyed playing around with a compass and bits of string.

If you want to draw a hex, take a compass, set it to any radius, and draw a circle. Still with the compass set to the same radius, step-off around the circumference of your circle. This done, take a pencil and straightedge, and link up alternate step-off marks until you have a six-pointed star. It's that simple—and quite enjoyable.

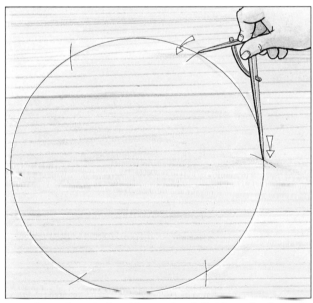

Drawing a hex-circle with a pair of dividers. See how the radius can be stepped-off six times around the circumference to create a six-pointed star.

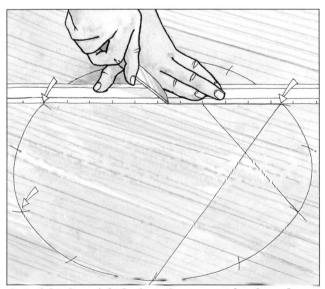

A straightedge might be just about any strip of wood, metal, or plastic.

A characteristic traditional six-pointed hex-star.

What makes Pennsylvania folk art painting so special, and what sets it apart from other European–American work, is that, while other European groups arrived in America and continued to work in an ever diminishing echo of the mother country tradition, the Pennsylvania painters went on to develop a uniquely vigorous, yet primitive, style that nevertheless reflected their new-world freedoms.

While the Pennsylvania folk artists favored motifs and designs that were broadly popular, we should bear in mind, as discussed in the first chapter, that almost every element in Pennsylvania painting—the designs and the colors—is thought to have some symbolic significance. For example, the colors red and yellow have to do with Donar, the god associated with marriage, the unicorn symbolized virginity and purity, the entwined flowers and tree-like forms symbolized the tree of life, the hearts symbolized love, heraldic lions had to do with power, and so forth.

PAINTING TECHNIQUES

The execution of the Pennsylvania designs is characterized by the breadth and vigor of the painting techniques utilized by the folk artists. We think that it is important to realize that any single piece of work—a chest design, or a painted box, or whatever—might be a composite of the application of three or four quite different techniques. So, for example, a chest might be colorwashed, rubbed, brushworked, stippled, vinegar painted, worked with brush-stroke flowers, and then glazed.

If we want to get inside the working mind of the Pennsylvania folk artist—to the extent that we can approach the decoration with confidence and a sense of enjoyment—then it is important that we have a good understanding of the various painting techniques that were used.

Colorwash

In the context of painting wood, a colorwash is no more or less than a very thin coat, or wash, of color. A colorwash gives a tint to the surface—like looking through colored sunglasses—without hiding the underlying texture of the wood. So, for example, if you lay a thin colorwash of green on knotty pine, the "soft" grain takes up the pigment at a greater rate than the "hard" grain, with the effect that the character of the grain is greatly enhanced and exaggerated.

By laying on a wash and then sanding through at areas that would naturally develop wear—around handles, along edges and corners—it is possible, if not overdone, to achieve a patina effect that suggests that the wood is old and worn, and/or exotic.

Although Pennsylvania painters did use all sorts of colorwash recipes—everything from thin washes of oil and pigment, glue sizing and pigment to mixtures of paste, milk, and burnt clay—we favor simply using pure pigment and water, usually mixed with a small dash of acrylic.

Our favorite recipe is to add the water to the color until we have the desired density of tone, and then to lay on the wash with a wide, flat brush. The water evaporates, and the pigment bleeds into the wood. Such a wash results in a thin, clear color.

If you are keen to discover new procedures and recipes, you could search around for likely pigments and run a series of trials. For example, just thinking of easy-to-find natural products, here is a short list of things you could try: tea, coffee, beetroot juice, berry juice, red wine, red clay, mustard powder, boiled onion skins, rust, extract from various fungi, and so forth. There are hundreds of possibilities. All you do is mix the pigment with water, brush the resultant liquid onto a small tile of wood, leave it to dry, label and date the sample, and place it in a sunlit window to see if it fades.

Milk Paint Colorwash

Of all the traditional Pennsylvania paint recipes, milk paint was one of the most popular. Although there are many bonafide accounts that describe milk or buttermilk paint being used—written in Colonial times right through to the nineteenth century—most of the accounts take if for granted that the reader knows quite a bit already of what they are discussing. So, for example, although the writer might describe in some detail that the coloring agent is ox blood, or brick dust, or walnut juice, it is taken for granted that the reader knows all about the milk part of the recipe. We are left to assume from these accounts that the milk part of the recipe must be so "easy, everyday, and obvious"—like making flour and water paste—that the writers thought it unnecessary to mention.

Working on the premise that milk paint uses easy-to-find everyday kitchen and dairy ingredients like, for example, fresh milk and blackberry juice, with maybe a dash of salt or even vinegar sprinkled in to stop the mixture going sour, we have experimented with all manner of recipes—with varying degrees of success. Our mixes might be graded from okay, usable, and pretty good to bad, very smelly, and just plain nasty.

One milk colorwash recipe with which we have *always* had success uses nonfat instant milk powder and acrylic color. The making couldn't be easier; all we do is add water to the powder until we have a sticky paste—a bit like condensed milk—and then we stir in acrylic paint and/or children's powder color paint/pigment until the color is "right." The more milk, the more cloudy the paint; the more pigment, the stronger the color. Such a mix makes a colorwash that dries to a beautiful, faded, antique, slightly sheeny translucent finish.

If you enjoy experimenting, then milk paint and washes can be amazing fun! You could try recipes with fresh milk, yogurt, canned condensed milk, and canned evaporated milk.

Be Warned Never make a milk mix and then leave it in the kitchen unattended. It looks too much like something to drink—a milk shake. Always *label* containers, use the paint as soon as possible after making, and then clean up.

Rubbing

Rubbing is a technique whereby a flat painted surface is tinted by the application of a thin coat of oil-based glaze. The simplest method is to stir a small dab of artist's quality oil-based color with a small quantity of clear varnish, thin the mix with mineral/white spirit, and then wipe on the resultant mix with a pad of lint-free cloth. A rubbed finish, or tint, produces a cloud-like blooming that suggests that the color has faded and aged.

The proportions of oil pigment to varnish, and varnish to thinner, are factors that control the density of color and the drying and flowing properties of the glaze.

Antiquing

Antiquing is easily achieved by mixing a small amount of artist's raw umber oil-based color with a small amount of clear varnish, thinning the mixture slightly with white/mineral spirit, and wiping or brushing it on as a glaze.

On wood—either unvarnished or varnished—we usually lay on a thin coat of the mix, rub it well into the surface, and let it dry. When it is dry, we then give the whole surface a very quick sanding with the finest-grade sandpaper, and lay on another coat. And so we continue, repeating the stages, until the desired depth of finish has been achieved. The buildup of color in corners, crevices, cracks, and dents only adds to the overall finish.

If you swap the umber ingredient for other colors—red, gold, or whatever—it is possible to achieve an exotic surface that looks as if it has been variously bleached by age, stained with copper verdigris, badly treated by being left in the damp, and so forth.

Varnishing

Old-time accounts of varnishing problems are fearsome. One early-nineteenth-century book lists just a few of the problems as follows: varnish is apt to crawl, run, sag, wrinkle, go silky, go seedy, sandy or specky, pit, have pin-holes, pock, blotch, sweat, deaden, "wither," "sadden," go tacky, craze, crackle, scale, go cloudy, fog, bloom, blister, "chill" . . . and so the list goes on. The good news is that, to a great extent, modern varnishes have all the qualities of old-time recipes, without the defects.

Keeping in mind that we are primarily after a lively naive gloss rather than a perfect piano-shine finish, we favor using high-shine yacht varnish, either straight from the can or modified with small amounts of thinner and/or artist's oil-based color.

Ideally varnishing should be done on a warm, dry, windless day. You have to ensure that the surface to be varnished is dry, clean, and free from dust, and you do have to use clean, dry, oil-free brushes—but all that apart, the task is as easy as pie.

In the context of varnishing a large chest in a well-ventilated workshop, for instance, we would—

• Set the chest on trestles or an old table—so that it is at a good working height.
• Wipe the chest over with a spirit-dampened lint-free cloth.
• Use a wide, soft-haired brush to lay the varnish on in swift, thin coats. If we wanted the varnish thinner, we would thin it with white/mineral spirit, and if we wanted it tinted, we might add a touch of artist's oil-based color.

And, just so that you can learn by our mistakes: We once varnished over an oiled surface with the effect that the varnish stayed tacky. Another time we used a really poor-grade brush with the effect that the surface was covered in loose brush hairs. And, then again, we had the "brilliant" idea of doing the varnishing out in the yard—in the sunshine. It's a great idea, except for the wind-driven dust, insects, nosy dogs, and low-flying birds!

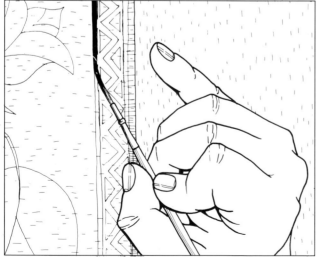

Using a striping brush—note how the small finger is used to brace and steady the moving hand.

One last bit of advice: We once bought a huge can of varnish, thinking that it was less expensive than lots of little cans. The only problem was—what with all the opening and closing of the can, and the can getting dented, and the lid not fitting because of the varnish buildup, and the skin on the varnish—we were soon left with half a can of unusable varnish! If you are trying to save money, our best advice is to purchase a number of small cans in bulk, and then to store them in a cool, fireproof, frost-free box in a garden workshop until needed.

Striping

Striping, also sometimes called pin-striping and/or lining, is the technique of painting continuous lines of a uniform width. In the context of Pennsylvania folk art paintings, the technique uses a soft-haired brush called a liner. Such brushes are characterized by having, depending on the type of brush and its usage, hairs from 1″ to 3″ long.

Old-time painters favored using the longest hairs possible, with a paint mix made from artist's oil-based color, white/mineral spirit, and clear varnish. Ideally the striping, or lining, paint needs to flow without being too thin or too thick. That said, we have happily worked with acrylic paint mixed with water.

In the context of striping a box, for instance, the surface is sanded to a smooth finish, the lines are set out with a pencil and ruler, the brush is loaded with paint, the full length of the head is set down on the surface, and the brush is drawn towards the painter's body. The secret of success lies in having a good brush, paint of the correct consistency, a well-prepared surface, and a steady, confident hand. Old-time stripers— the professionals who lined just about everything from wagons and chairs to wooden boxes and tin trays— declared that the surface to be worked needed to be prepared with at least three or more coats of high-shine varnish. The idea was, no doubt, that the smooth surface encouraged easy, flowing work.

We have two things to say on this: we personally are not overly keen on seeing too much striping; and we much prefer a striped line to start and finish with a taper. To our taste and inclination, a swift, uneven line adds character.

If you want to become wonderfully skilled at striping, our advice is to practise, and then to practise, and then to practise some more.

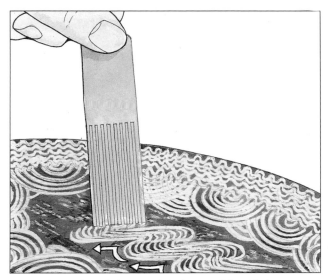

A small metal graining comb being used in this instance to create a random-pattern design.

The metal comb scrapes through the varnish glaze to reveal the color of the underlying flat paint.

Graining

Traditionally, graining was a technique of variously disguising and dressing up inexpensive base woods so that they had the appearance of being exotic and expensive. At its most basic, the technique involves laying on a flat ground coat, giving the dry ground a coat of glaze or colored varnish, and then combing through to topcoat to reveal the color of the underlying paint. By laying on a dark red ground, for instance, and a dark brown topcoat and then combing, you finish up with a dark brown surface that looks to have a red grain.

Although in the eighteenth and nineteenth centuries the art of graining evolved into a technique that concentrated almost entirely on dressing up one type of wood to look like another—so that the finish was truly indistinguishable from the real thing—the Pennsylvania painters were more interested in achieving a swift, dramatic finish. Old pieces of Pennsylvania grained furniture are characterized by having wildly grained surfaces that in no way try to mimic the graining pattern of real woods. So, for example, there are chests with huge swirls of red and orange graining, cupboards with knot designs as big as dinner plates, and so forth.

As with many traditional painting techniques, the only way to get to know about graining is to sit down with a suitable piece of furniture for experimentation, and maybe one or two color shots showing museum pieces, and then to have a go. When we first started, we were presented with the problem of having three doors all looking into a hallway. All three doors had been grained sometime at the beginning of the nineteenth century. Two of them were in good condition, while one had—we imagined—suffered at the hands of some long-gone, blowtorch-toting, possibly demented resident with an odd sense of decoration. We saw our task as figuring out how to "restore" the damaged door so that it matched the other two.

After a deal of picking away at the paint layers, we soon discovered that the door had a matt, biscuit-buff-brown undercoat, followed by a matt, bright orange middle coat, finished by a dark brown gloss topcoat. Anyway, to cut a long story short, we experimented on pieces of scrap plywood with various combinations, combs, and drying times until we had a good match. At the end of all our trial-and-error, varnish-covered struggles, we came away, at least, with a few sound pieces of advice to pass on to others. The middle coat needs to be bright enough to shine through the topcoat, the drying time between laying on the top glaze and combing is critical, and, most important of all, it's essential to have a practice run on some scrap wood.

The secret of graining is deciding just when the top glaze is ready to be combed. Do it too early and the glaze continues to flow—do it too late and the surface is impossible to comb.

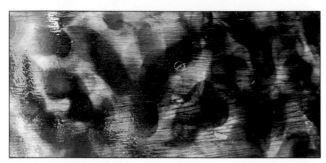

Candle marbling—the candle smoke passes into the varnish to create a shiny, dappled effect.

Candle Marbling

Candle marbling, sometimes called smoke marbling, is a delightfully simple and effective technique that results in a beautiful dappled finish. It is found primarily on small items that easily can be hand-held, such as wall boxes, chairs, bellow fronts, and the like. The technique is achieved as follows—

• Give the item to be decorated a good bright ground coat—such as bright green, red, or orange—either a flat paint or a wash, and let it dry.
• Cover the ground coat with clear varnish.
• When the varnish is tack-dry, pass a lighted candle about an inch or so away from the surface so that the smoke leaves black marks.

It does sound a bit messy and hit and miss, but the wonderful thing is that the resultant clouds, streaks, and trails of black soot left by the smoke somehow or other pass into the varnish to become permanent.

Vinegar painting—the vinegar and varnish mix "crawls" to create a characteristic wood-grain effect.

Having said that it's easy—and it really is—you do have to take care not to pass the candle flame so close that you blister the varnish, and not to start the smoking until the varnish is tack-dry. This last point is particularly important, because, if you start the smoking too soon, the varnish will light up like crêpes flambés—not a pretty sight.

We recommend, especially if you are a beginner, that you try this technique out in the garden or yard. Always be sure to keep the lighted candle well away from white/mineral spirit, turpentines, open cans of varnish, and the like.

Vinegar Painting

Vinegar painting, sometimes also described as vinegar graining and putty graining, is, as these names suggest, a method of graining and texturing wood. The technique is most commonly found on Pennsylvania chests, chairs, and boxes from the nineteenth century. The surface is characterized by being dark brown with whorls and twists of pattern.

The technique couldn't be easier; all you do is paint on a flat ground coat—such as a mellow or buff yellow—wait for it to dry, cover it with a mixture made from varnish, burnt-umber artist's oil-based color, and vinegar, and then variously stroke and texture the vinegar coat with a comb and/or a twist of putty.

When we first saw the recipe, we thought that it would be impossible to stir in the water-based vinegar with the oil-based varnish. The exciting thing is, however, that once the mix has been brushed on, it slowly starts to "crawl," with the effect that the surface takes on a characteristic wood-like pattern even before you begin the texturing.

Vinegar painting can also be achieved by laying on a ground coat and then painting on a mixture of malt vinegar and watercolor pigment. The effect is much the same as that from using a vinegar and varnish mix—the same color—the only real difference being that the paint doesn't crawl. In our experience, however, we haven't had much luck with the water-based mix—consequently we prefer using the oil and vinegar recipe. As with other slightly unpredictable techniques, it's always a good idea to have a tryout on a sheet of scrap wood. We say this because the drying times vary: plenty of time with the vinegar to varnish mix; but for the pigment and water the drying period was so swift that there wasn't enough time to complete the combing.

Scumbling

There are two different painting techniques that are both known as scumbling—one uses a transparent oil glaze over a flat ground color, and the other uses a flat, opaque paint over a bright and shiny ground color. In the context of Pennsylvania folk art, we are only interested in oil-glaze scumbling.

The scumbled finish—most commonly found on Pennsylvania chests and cupboards from the nineteenth century—is primarily characterized by being shiny, with the marks of the brush and/or pad being clearly visible. The effect is achieved by laying on a flat opaque ground coat—typically straw-yellow or yellow ochre—letting it dry, and then brushing or dabbing it with a thin mix of clear varnish, umber artist's oil-based color, and turpentine. By adjusting the color of the ground coat, and/or the color of the glaze, it is possible to achieve a whole variety of effects.

This is one of those techniques that is best used to give character and texture to an otherwise dull and uninteresting ground, and/or to a ground coat that you think is in some way damaged or less than perfect. For example, let's say that, having painstakingly brushed on a ground coat of green, it dries out to rather an unpleasant, sharp pea-green. All you do is tone it all down with a coat of scumble glaze. Or then again, let's say that having completed a design—the undercoat, the design details, and all the rest—you find that one or other of the colors is so jarring that it causes an imbalance. All you do is lay a scumble glaze over the whole works. The glaze tones down the colors much as if they are being viewed through a filter or a sheet of colored film.

Sponging

Sponging, also known variously as mottling and stippling, is a paint texture most commonly found on boxes and chests from the eighteenth and nineteenth centuries.

The technique involves using a sponge, a brush, or even a dry corn cob to dab-texture the ground color. The object to be decorated is first painted with a light ground color, left until the paint is completely dry, and then textured with a paint or glaze of a different color. So, for example, you might paint a box dark blue with panels of off-white, and then sponge-texture the dark blue ground with a slightly lighter blue.

Feather Painting

Feather painting, found on Pennsylvania chests of the nineteenth century, involves much the same technique as scumbling. The only real difference is that the top glaze is drawn off and textured with a feather rather than a brush or pad.

The piece is first painted with a light, bright, flat, opaque ground color—say straw-yellow or buff—the dry ground is painted over with a transparent glaze mix of varnish and turpentine tinted with a dab of artist's oil-based color, and then, finally, the glazed surface is brushed, patterned, and variously textured with the feather. By using different sizes of feather, and trailing and combing the feather, it is possible to achieve some very exciting hooked, curled, and coiled designs.

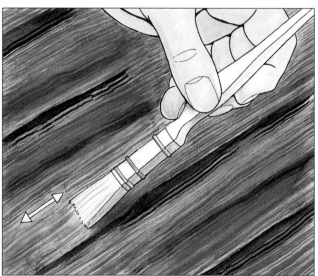

Tortoiseshelling—use a dry brush to stroke the surface first one way and then the other until the colors merge and blend.

Tortoiseshelling

Tortoiseshell decoration is a mottled brown and yellow effect found most commonly on boxes, chests, and interior detailing. With the technique of tortoiseshelling, the surface is given a flat undercoat, streaked with oil-based paint and varnish, and then stroked with a dry brush. The colors merge and blend with the effect that they bleed into one another to give a mottled shell-like texture and coloration.

— 1 —
Pennsylvania Floor Hex

THE EARLY PENNSYLVANIA painters were very fond of hex motifs. They painted huge hex circle-stars on barns, hex patterns on floor cloths, running hex designs on walls, single, small hex circles on dower chests, and so on. They painted hex designs on just about everything and anything that took their fancy.

Traditionally, floors were decorated with hex circles—usually set out with a compass, but sometimes with a stencil—the idea being that the overall design imitated fancy earthenware tiles and/or carpet patterns. We have the feeling, however, that for many of the old-time painters, the magic of hex motifs had to do with the way they could be easily set out with nothing more complicated than a pair of compasses or dividers—or even a piece of string—and a straightedge. They didn't need to know about math or figures, they just got in there and watched the motifs grow.

1-1   Project picture. The finished hex-circle.

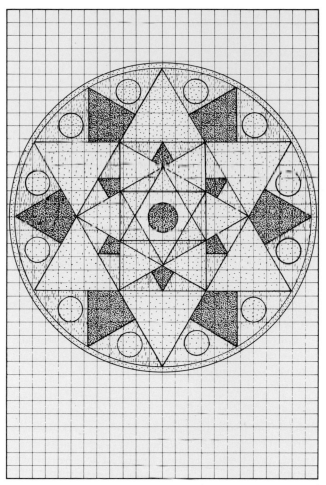

1-2   Working drawing.

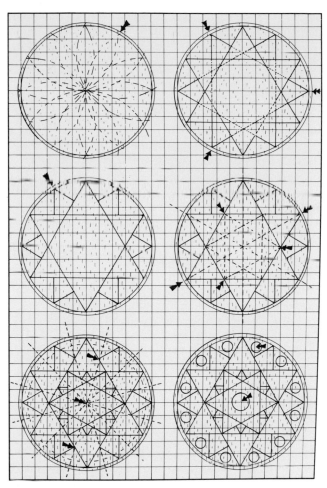

1-3   Grid design. The working stages—from left to right, top to bottom.

A good deal of the joy and pleasure of painting hex circle-star motifs, we have found, lies not so much in the actual painting, but rather in the compass work and in the general setting out.

If you look at our illustrations (see **1-1**), you will see that we chose to use a hex circle to decorate a small area of bare, board floor. If you look at the design grid and working drawings (see **1-2** and **1-3**), you will see that, once we have scribed out the large circle and the first six step off arcs, then the rest of the design is set out with the straightedge.

Another fascination lies in the somewhat mystifying nature of hex motifs in that they always appear to be innately balanced and well proportioned. It doesn't matter how big or how small the circles, whether you divide the circumference with a compass and link selected points to make a six- or twelve-pointed star, and then maybe go on to subdivide areas; the final design is always pleasing to the eye.

CHOOSING THE PAINTS, COLORS, MATERIALS, AND BRUSHES

Although we have chosen to decorate a floor, if you want to use the technique to decorate wall boards or a cupboard door or whatever, then no problem; you simply stay with the general method and modify the stages to suit. The principal thing to bear in mind when decorating floors is that the finished design has to be protected with varnish. Plan on at least two coats of varnish, applied 24 hours apart.

The technique uses a coat of tinted varnish glaze to seal and stain the bare boards, acrylic colors for the design, and two or more coats of tinted varnish glaze to finish.

We made use of a pair of dividers, a knife, and a straightedge for setting out, a large household brush for the varnishing, and small, sable brushes for the decoration.

MATERIALS

You will need—

• an area of bare floorboards to decorate—best if they are old, stained, and worn
• a pair of large fixed-leg dividers or compasses
• a sharp-point knife—we use an old hunting knife
• a pack of graded sandpapers
• flat, acrylic paints in the colors bright orange, red, and umber
• a couple of soft-haired, sable watercolor brushes—a broad- and a fine-point
• a can of clear varnish
• a quantity of mineral/white spirit for thinning the varnish
• a tube of umber artist's quality oil color
• a collection of throwaway cans and jars
• all the usual around-the-house items like newspapers, running water, old cloths, and various spoons for mixing and stirring

PROJECT STAGES

Preparation

Having studied the design (see **1-2**) and organized your tools and materials, then comes the not-so-easy task of preparing the floor. It is best to start by making sure that there is plenty of ventilation and good light and that the floor is in suitable condition. You also need to figure out just how you, your family and friends, the children, the dog, and the cat, such as there are, are going to maneuver once the floor has been varnished.

Be Warned Our motif took about three hours to set out and decorate, and two days for the varnish to dry.

Set nails below the surface, scrape off such things as old paint, dog hairs, oil, floor wax, and the like, and then sand the wood to a smooth finish. Don't worry about old varnish or general wear-and-tear marks—they add character. Just make sure that the boards are free from substances that might interfere with the finish. Clean up the dust, and wipe the surface over with a spirit-dampened cloth.

Finally, warn friends and family about what you are doing, and then the fun can begin.

Special Tip Be very wary about varnishing a floor that you think might have been oiled. Oil slows down the drying time!

Laying On the Ground

Decant what you calculate as enough varnish for the area to be decorated, and add a small "worm" of umber artist's oil-based color, as well as a small amount of mineral/white spirit. Gently stir the ingredients. When you have achieved a good mix and tested it for color—it needs to be smooth running and a warm gold-brown color—seal the floor with a single coat. When the varnish is completely dry, give it a quick sanding with a fine-grade sandpaper, clean up the dust, and lay on another coat of varnish.

Setting Out the Design

Study the working drawing (see **1-3**). Take your tools—the dividers, knife, and straightedge—and get to work. Start by fixing the dividers to the radius of your desired circle.

Special Tip If the dividers are loose-legged, and the radius "creeps," then the design will get messed up. If you use dividers with screw-fixed legs, then you won't have problems.

Spike the dividers down to make a center point, and scribe out a single clean circle (see **1-3**, top left). Next, spike the point on the circumference, and swing the dividers around in an arc to mark the circumference at two cross-over points. Repeat this procedure to mark six step-offs around the circle (see **1-4**). Take the dividers, establish the midway point between any two neighboring step-offs—this is easily done by trial and error—and then repeat the procedure as already described. You should finish up with twelve equidistant step-offs around the circumference.

With the twelve marks in place, take the straightedge and the knife, and use alternate marks to carefully set out the six-pointed star (see **1-5**). It's important that the marks are clean and crisp; so get it right the first time around. When you are happy with the star, then repeat the procedure with the other step-offs; only this time simply draw in the star points. If all is going well, you should have a six-pointed star with secondary points between each of its points (see **1-3**, middle left).

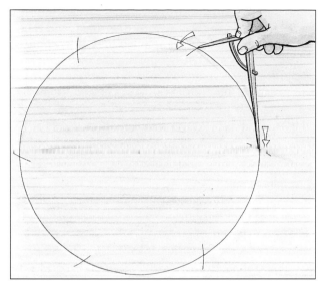

1-4 *Fix the six points by stepping-off the radius around the circumference.*

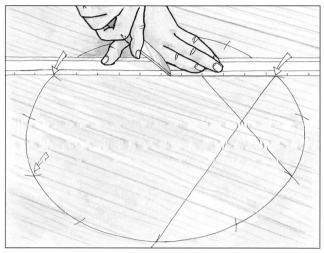

1-5 *Use the knife and the straightedge to link up the step-off points.*

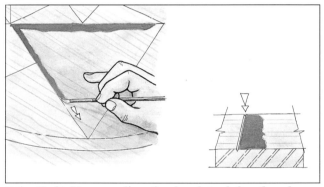

1-6 *(Left) Use a medium-fine brush to define the edges, and then use a bigger brush to block in. (Right) The scored line will stop the paint from bleeding along the run of the grain.*

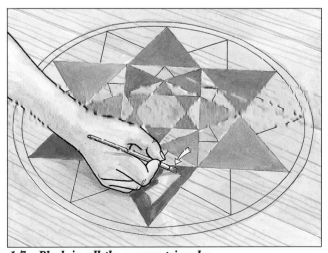

1-7 *Block in all the orange triangles.*

Having achieved the twelve-pointed form with a six-sided shape at its center—called a hexagon—use the six points of the hexagon to repeat the star-drawing procedure as already described. Continue until you have, as it were, a star within a star within a star. Note how the middle star only has six points. Last, draw a slightly larger circle so that the total design is contained by a border.

Special Tip If you have doubts about the procedure, then have a tryout on a sheet of paper. It's important that the floor motif be clean-cut and positive; so it's best to make all your mess-ups on paper.

Painting the Design

With the total hex-circle nicely set out, take the bright orange color, and decant what you think is enough for the task ahead. It's better to have too much rather than too little. Add a small amount of acrylic umber to tone down the color, and stir to mix.

Take the muddied bright orange and your sable brushes, and set to work blocking in all the triangles that go to make up the design. The best method is to use the fine-point brush to paint up to the scratched line (see **1-6**, top), and then block in with the large brush. The scratched line will stop the color from bleeding along the grain (see **1-6**, bottom). Block in the six large outer triangles with orange (see **1-7**).

1-8 *Block in the red diamond points.*

1-9 *Finally, block in the red circle in the middle and the outer ring of twelve circles.*

When you are happy with the orange blocks, muddy the red slightly in the way already described, and then block in the red star points as illustrated. If by chance you make a mess-up anywhere along the way, then immediately wipe the paint away with a damp cloth and start over. Continue until you have painted in all the red shapes (see **1-8**).

When the paint is dry, use the straightedge and pencil to fix the centers of the ring of small between-point circles, and draw them with the dividers (see **1-3**, bottom). Draw a single circle at the center of the hex. Finally, block in the single circle with red and the twelve outer circles with orange (see **1-9**).

Finishing

Finishing couldn't be easier; all you do is make sure that the acrylic colors are completely dry, remove the dust by wiping over the design with a spirit-dampened cloth, and then lay on at least a couple of coats of your tinted varnish glaze. Don't forget to allow 24 hours between coats, and to give the varnish a quick sanding with the finest-grade paper or steel wool before laying on another coat.

AFTERTHOUGHTS

• If you are a beginner, it might be just as well to spend time, prior to the project, playing with a compass and drawing out hex-stars.
• If at the end of your efforts the colors look a bit harsh, then lay on extra coats of varnish glaze.
• Spirit varnish gives off a potentially toxic vapor—especially if it's being used in a small, enclosed, hot room. It is always best to have all the doors and windows open, and to remove plants, pets, and children.
• **Be Warned** If you varnish on a humid or damp day, there is a chance that the finish will cloud or bloom. It is best to varnish on a dry, breezy day.
• **Be Warned** Spirit varnish is highly flammable. On no account work by candlelight, smoke while you are varnishing, or have any other open flame in the room.

—2—
Fraktur Flower Hex

MANY AUTHORITIES CONSIDER that fraktur illustration is the primary source of and key to Pennsylvania folk art designs and motifs. It is thought that many of the traditional patterns and designs that we see painted on just about everything from barns and brooms to boxes and headboards have their root in fraktur greeting cards, calligraphic writing sheets, and certificates.

Fraktur drawing and painting, as practised by the Pennsylvania Germans, was/is the art and craft of calligraphic manuscript illumination. That is to say, Gothic type is formally written with goose-quill pens, and then selected letters, and the borders in and around the page, are decorated with stylized ink drawings and patterns.

Fraktur, as seen in eighteenth- and nineteenth-century Pennsylvania, found expression in just about everything from baptismal, marriage, and death certificates to bookplates, house blessings, and love tokens.

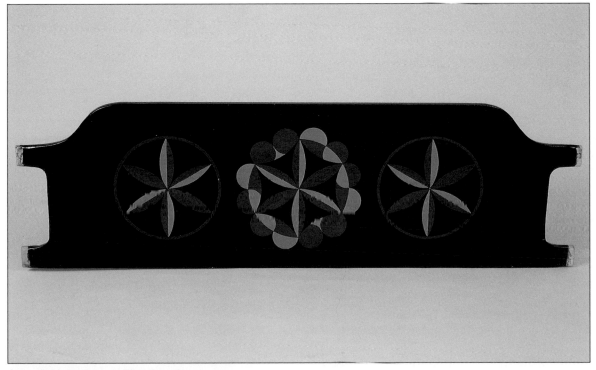

2-1   Project picture. The three-hex design.

39

Our compass flower hex (see **2-1**) draws its inspiration from a Pennsylvania German fraktur birth certificate dated 1808. Apart from the usual written details, the design includes three really splendid compass-drawn hex flowers. The wonderful thing about compass motifs is that they can be drawn easily even by so called nonartists. Or to put it more directly, if you can hold a compass and draw a circle, then there's no excuse at all for opting out of this project!

Although we have chosen to decorate a headboard, we could just as well have gone for a box, chair splat, or something else. Our primary concern in this project rests not so much with the context of the decoration, but rather with the actual techniques—meaning drawing the circles and painting.

CHOOSING THE PAINTS, COLORS, MATERIALS, AND BRUSHES

Keeping in mind that our principal interest has to do with method rather than context, the techniques call for a coat of acrylic paint to color and texture the wood, a tinted varnish glaze to seal and stain the surface, acrylic colors for the design, and two or more coats of tinted varnish glaze to finish.

We use a pair of dividers for setting out the designs, a medium-size household brush for the varnishing, and small sable brushes for the decoration.

MATERIALS

You will need—

• a large, solid-wood surface to decorate—we have chosen a headboard
• a pair of large fixed-leg dividers
• a pair of fixed-leg compasses
• a pencil and ruler
• a pack of graded sandpapers
• a small amount of leftover acrylic paint in such colors as grey, umber, and blue-black
• flat acrylic paints in the colors blue, cream, and brown for the circles
• a can of clear varnish
• a tube of artist's quality umber oil-based paint
• a household paintbrush about 1″ wide
• a couple of soft-haired sable watercolor brushes—a broad- and a fine-point
• a quantity of mineral/white spirit for thinning the varnish

• a collection of throwaway cans and jars
• all the usual around-the-house items like newspapers, running water, old cloths, and various spoons for mixing and stirring
• a quantity of furniture wax polish

PROJECT STAGES

Preparation

Working on the premise that you are decorating solid, relatively new, wood—rather than, say, particleboard—take your selected piece, and make sure that it's in good condition, stable, and worth decorating. Remove hardware, fill holes, scrape off flaky paint, and generally bring the surface to good order. For example, our headboard had, at some time or other, been painted, plus it was threatening to split along its length, so we removed the paint and screwed and glued battens across the back and sanded the wood to a smooth finish.

When you have achieved a good clean surface, then comes the interesting and somewhat contrary task of giving it "character." The object of the exercise is to build up color and texture so that when the wood has been glazed, decorated, and reglazed, the texture and color suggest that it has age and a past. This stage is particularly important if you are working with a completely new piece.

Take a cloth and the leftovers of acrylic paint—grey, blue-black, and umber—and work the paint into the grain. Concentrate your efforts on and around the area that is to be decorated. That is, rub the paint into the grain, build up layers of paint, and generally dab and daub the paint to create the impression of past layered decoration. This done, wait for the paint to dry completely, and then use the finest-grade sandpaper to cut through the paint at wear points.

Laying On the Ground

Decant enough varnish for four or more coats into a throwaway container—two coats to start the project and two to finish. Add a small "worm" of raw umber oil-based paint and a dash of mineral/white spirit, and stir the mix together. Don't worry about air bubbles and the like, just make sure that the oil-based paint is well mixed in. This done, give the workpiece a single, well-brushed coat of the resultant glaze, and let it dry.

With the glaze completely dry, take the fine-grade sandpaper, and once again sand the wood at natural

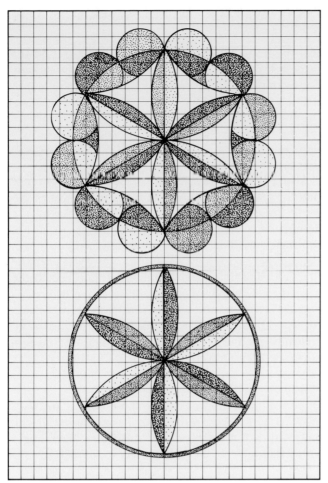

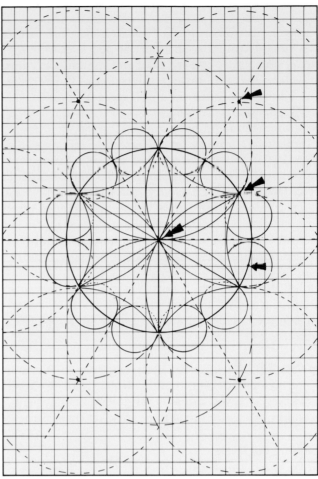

2-2 *Working drawing—no scale needed. Note how both hex-circles are based on the same radius. See also how the color sequence runs around the design.*

2-3 *Working drawing—the hex layout, showing the important plotting points.*

wear areas. Finally, lay on another coat of varnish glaze, and let it dry. If all is well and as described, the underlying paint should appear as a subtle texture, an indefinable shadow under the glaze, that creates the impression that there are past decorations. You should be able to feel the texture under your fingertips.

Setting Out the Design

When you have studied the working drawings (see 2-2 and 2-3) to the extent that you have a clear understanding of how the flower hex circles are drawn, decide whereabouts on your piece the circles need to be positioned and how large you want the circles to be, and then fix the center points accordingly.

Having noted how the two circles are based on the same radius, set the dividers to a radius that suits your chosen piece, and tighten up the screw so that the legs are going to stay put.

Special Tip It's important that the legs of the dividers stay fixed the required radius. If the legs creep apart, then the project will be messed up.

One circle at a time, spike the dividers on the center point, and scribe out a clear circle. Next, spike the point on the circumference—at 12 o'clock high—and scribe out an arc that starts and finishes on the circumference. This done, and using each arc in turn as the starting point for the next, repeat the procedure around the circle until you have drawn the characteristic six-petal flower form (see 2-3). Draw out the six-petal form for all three circles.

With all three circles in place, use a pencil and straightedge to give each petal a midline. Having taken the compasses and fixed them to the same radius as the dividers, go back to the central circle—the one with the fancy edge—and extend the petal arcs so

41

that neighboring arcs intersect at points outside the circle. This done, take a pencil and straightedge, and draw lines that run through the center of the circle to link up opposite intersections. If you have done it correctly, you will see that the straight lines fix the halfway point between neighboring petals.

Spike the dividers on the arc intersections—the ones that occur well outside the circle—and scribe out arcs that run from petal point to petal point to create petal shapes that run around the circumference. Finally, using the various lines and points as guides, reset your dividers, and scribe out the small circles that run around the circumference. If you have any doubts as to the drawing order, refer to the working drawing (see **2-3**). Note the primary plotting points—the center of the circle, the points on the circumference where the radius arc intersects, the arc intersection outside the circle, and the centers of the little circles (see also **2-4**).

Special Tip In many ways, describing how to draw the flower hex circles is more difficult than actually doing it. However, if you are a never-done-it-before beginner, then it's a good idea to practise on paper first.

Painting the Design

Once you have drawn the three-circle design, and maybe even modified the circles to suit your own fancies, then have a look again at the working drawings and the project picture to see how we have used the three colors in such a way that like colors never touch. For example, if you look at the large flower, you will see that with the small circles that run around the circumference and the petal forms we have carefully set out the colors so that there is an ordered 1-2-3, 1-2-3 sequence. It's best to pencil-label the various areas so that you know what color goes where.

Using a fine-point sable brush, take one or other of the colors—cream, for instance—and go over the whole three-circle design, edging in the blocks that are designated to be painted cream. It's very easy to make a mistake and fill in the wrong block; so take your time. Use a larger brush to block in the color. Wait until the first color has dried completely, and then repeat the procedure with the other two colors. When two colors butt against each other, spend time aiming for a clean-cut smooth line (see **2-5**). If your brush hand is at all unsteady, then use the other hand as a brace and support (see **2-6** and **2-7**).

Finishing

Once you have blocked in the three colors, and variously painted on second coats to cover, tidied up the lines with a fine-point brush, and wiped back edges with a damp cloth, let the paints dry completely.

2-5   *Make sure that the first color is completely dry before you lay down the adjacent color. Pull the brush towards your body, with your brush hand to the side of the line.*

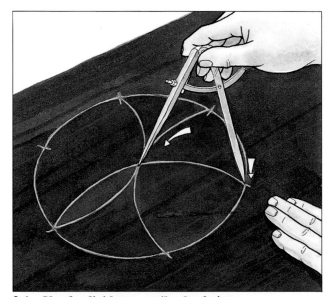

2-4   *Use the dividers to scribe the design.*

2-6   *It is sometimes helpful to support and steady your working hand—especially when painting arcs and circles.*

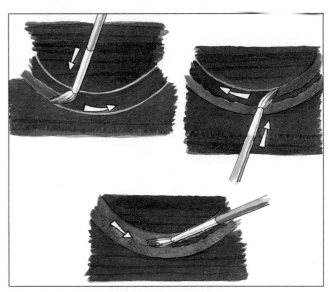

2-7   *Paint the outer circle in three stages—with the tip of the brush pointing towards the drawn line, first paint one edge and then the other (top left and right), and, finally, block in missing areas (bottom).*

With the colors in place, go back to the beginning and repeat the varnish glaze with two more coats; that is, lay on a coat of glaze, let it dry, sand it slightly, and lay on the second coat.

Finally, when the last coat of glaze is good and "squeaky" dry, give the whole works a coat of furniture wax and burnish it to a high-sheen finish.

AFTERTHOUGHTS

• When you are using the dividers, you have to be very careful that you don't peel up the varnish glaze. To this end, it's important that the divider points are sharpened to a needle point.

• If you want to go for a hotter glaze color, consider adding a worm of red oil-based paint to the varnish and umber mix.

• If you want to tone down your acrylic colors before painting, then add a little dab of raw umber acrylic to each color.

• Although, when we set out to decorate the headboard, we envisaged having large bold circles, we would now, on consideration, go for smaller circles—and maybe have six motifs at half the size.

—3—
Patriotic Eagle Dower Chest

THIS PROJECT—THE complete eagle panel—draws its inspiration from a dower chest, dated 1816, and signed on the scroll "Wilhelm Wagoner." This particular chest is extra special in that the design is a rich and dynamic mix of the old-world German and new-world American. On the one hand, there is the patriotic and heraldic American eagle, complete with scroll and shield—part of the Great Seal of The United States, first used in 1782—and then again, there are the stylized German hex circles and the tulips, and the even more ancient and pagan swastika-hex circles. This design is significant in that it marks the crossover period, when the Old World was fast being overtaken by the New. So, for example, although the itinerant decorators were still using the old symbols and motifs, they had very little understanding of their symbolic relevance. And anyway, the painters were more than happy to chop up and change traditional design layouts to suit changing tastes and fashions.

3-1 Project picture—showing the whole chest.

44

3-2 *Working drawing—the scale is approximately two grid squares to 1". Note that, apart from the eagle's head and the banner, the panel is symmetrical.*

From the painter's viewpoint, this is a great project (see **3-1**). The design is punchy and powerful, the colors are strong, and the finished chest is, by any standards, a potent statement. If you want to make a bold "I love America" declaration, and if you like dramatic heraldic imagery, then this is the project for you. And last, but not least, the scroll allows you to personalize the design with a name—wonderful!

CHOOSING THE PAINTS, COLORS, MATERIALS, AND BRUSHES

A good part of the strength of this design has to do with the self-imposed limited choice of colors and the blended-color technique. That is to say, we have selected four traditional colors—brick red, cream, blue-black, and white—then achieved subtle variations by mixing one with another. So, for example, within the swastika circles two of the details are painted straight colors—brick red and blue-black—whereas the other

two details are painted brick red plus a dash of cream, and blue-black plus cream. Working in this way, we have increased the range, while at the same time ensuring a balance.

We use a flat, watercolor wash brush for the ground, and various-size sables for the details.

MATERIALS

You will need

• a good size chest to decorate—ours has a front panel measuring 32" long and 20" high
• a pack of graded sandpapers
• a quantity of flat vinyl/latex paint in a soft cream color
• a sheet each of workout and tracing paper—to fit the size of your selected chest
• a pencil and ruler
• a pair of fixed-leg compasses

45

3-3   Use a large flat wash brush to lay on the ground color on the panel. Work in the direction of the grain, and lay on one or more coats for a flat, dense cover.

• a flat, soft-haired watercolor wash brush at about 2″ wide
• a selection of sable brushes, in sizes ranging from medium to fine
• a quantity of beeswax furniture polish
• all the usual around-the-house items like newspapers, running water, old cloths, and various spoons for mixing

PROJECT STAGES

Preparation

Take your chosen chest, and spend time removing all the hardware. Unscrew handles and catches, and generally remove the clutter.

With all the fittings out of the way, spend time removing the paint. We prefer to use a scraper, or even a blowtorch, rather than a chemical stripper. We say this because not only are some strippers so powerful that they leave the wood looking bleached and lifeless, but even worse, their smell and general unpleasantness makes them completely user-unfriendly!

Take a fine-grade sandpaper and sand the wood down to a smooth finish. When you have removed the paint—without, we hope, too many scrapes and burns to you and the chest—mix a little of the brick-red acrylic, and wipe the resultant wash over the surface of the wood. Use a cloth, and continue rubbing away until the wood takes on an all-over blush of red. When you have, perhaps, added a little more wash for a stronger color, and more or less rubbed the paint dry,

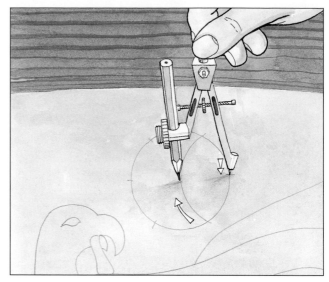

3-4   Use a pair of fixed-leg compasses to draw out the hex-circles. Make sure that the compass stays at the same radius throughout.

use the fine-grade sandpaper to sand away the whiskers and nibs of grain.

Laying On the Ground

Having taken extra care with the preparation—because after all it is the wood that is on show—draw the design to size (see **3-2**), and make a clear tracing. This done, establish the center of the chest side by drawing crossed diagonals, and then draw in a vertical centerline and a base line.

With the guidelines in place, and, having used a soft pencil to rework the lines at the back of the tracing, align the tracing and use the straightedge and either a hard pencil or a ballpoint pen to press-transfer the shape of the panel onto the wood. It's important that the panel shape is accurately drawn out; so spend time getting it right.

When you have double-checked that the panel shape is nigh on perfect, take the cream vinyl/latex paint and the flat wash brush, and set to work laying on the ground. Use the brush much as you would a striping brush. That is, load the brush with paint, set the head down within the drawn line, and then drag the brush along and up to the line to achieve a crisp clean edge to the panel shape (see **3-3**).

Last, when you have established a clean profile, and not forgetting to give a light sanding between coats, lay on one or more coats of paint to cover.

3-5 *Painting the black—use a fine brush for the outline and a larger brush to block in. Make sure that the paint is smooth and free-running.*

3-6 *Use a fine-point brush to paint in the thin red color.*

Setting Out the Design

Check that the paint is good and dry, then realign the tracing with the panel, fix it in place with tabs of masking tape, and set to work press-transferring the lines of the design onto the cream ground. When you come to the hex circles at either side of the eagle's head, do no more than establish the center points. And then again, with the two swastika-hex circles, fix the center point and draw in the four arms, but leave the circle undrawn.

When you have transferred all of the primary motifs, remove the tracing paper, use the pencil and ruler to draw the border line around the panel, and use the pair of compasses to finish the circles (see **3-4**). Use the radius-arc technique to draw out the six-petal flower hex in the two upper circles (refer to projects one and two).

Painting the Design

By the time you get to the painting stage, the worst is over and you are on the home run. Set out your four acrylic colors—brick red, blue-black, cream, and white—and use the sable brushes of your choice to edge in the details and to block in (see **3-5**). The best procedure is to deal with one color at a time; so you might block in all the blue-black, then all the brick red, and so on. As to the actual technique of laying on the colors, there is not much to say other than that

you should use the fine-point brush to line in the drawn lines, and then follow through with a larger brush for the blocks of color.

What we did was block in the blue-black, then the brick red (see **3-6**), then the white, and then added a dash of cream to the brick red for the pale brick red color, and so on. For the shield we painted the wide brick-red bands first, and then finished up with the blue-black striping (see **3-7**).

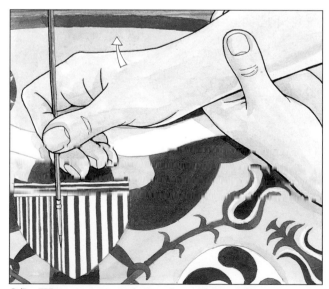

3-7 *When you are painting the stripes, support the wrist of the brush hand, and try all the while to make a single, confident "dragging" stroke.*

3-8   Use a fine-grade sandpaper to lightly blur and cut through the painted surface—work in the direction of the grain.

The design finished, stand back and give it a critical once-over. As needed, use the fine brush to adjust lines and details. Last, paint a name on the scroll, and sign and date the underside of the chest.

Finishing

Wait for the paint to dry completely, and then set to work with the fine-grade sandpaper and a dry cloth (see **3-8**). With the sandpaper in one hand and the cloth in the other, the technique is to rub the whole face of the chest down to a smooth, slightly blurred finish, and then burnish. If you are doing it right, the sanding will scour and cut through the various layers of paint, and the cloth will then rub the multicolored paint dust into the resultant sanded texture. The more you sand and burnish, the more faded and burnished the finished design.

Finally, when you have taken the finish as far as you want, wipe away the dust with a clean cloth, give the whole works a generous coat of clear wax polish, and burnish the surface to a deep-sheen finish.

AFTERTHOUGHTS

• If you enjoy Pennsylvania painting, then our best advice is to always be on the lookout for likely items to decorate. We found our chest dumped in a rubbish bin. It has cast brass handles, it is beautifully made, and remains of paper labels bear witness that it has been to Simla in India and suggest that it is at least one hundred years old. The moral of this tale is that there are still bargains to be had—if you keep your eyes open!

• If you have a fancy to continue doing Pennsylvania painting over the long haul, then get yourself a sketch/scrap book, visit museums, and start collecting photographs and making sketches of the many wonderfully bold designs.

• On the original chest, the eagle looks to the right. We didn't want to be accused of trying to pass our chest off as the real thing, so we changed the eagle so that it looks to the left.

—4—
Vinegar Painting an Oval Box

VINEGAR PAINTING, SOMETIMES also described by the old-timers as vinegar or putty graining, is a beautifully swift and effective way of painting wood. The technique involves laying on a flat base coat, covering the dry flat coat with a mix of paint and vinegar, and then variously making marks on/through the vinegar coat to reveal the underlying flat color.

That the Pennsylvania painters were very fond of using this technique is clear, because they used it to decorate just about everything, from small boxes and chests to large projects like wardrobes, chest of drawers, and room interiors. That said, we suspect that a good part of its popularity is due to its being very cheap to make and very swift to apply. What could be easier?—a light-colored coat of flat paint for the ground (no doubt they used leftovers from other projects)—under a mix of varnish and vinegar. Some old accounts describe using stale beer rather than vinegar. Exactly how much beer was allowed to go stale is something again!

4-1 Project picture—the finished box.

It's worth mentioning that although we mix the vinegar with a varnish glaze, some traditional recipes also describe using a flat water paint mix.

Having looked at the project picture (see **4-1**) and the other illustrations to see how we have chosen to do the texturing with a metal graining comb, there's nothing to say that you can't try out various alternative traditional techniques. For example, you might use a screw of newspaper, a wad of Plasticine or putty, or just about anything that makes an interesting mark.

The secret of the technique lies not so much in the actual mix, or even in the layering of the paint and the vinegar, but rather in the color of the underlying flat paint and the timing of the texturing. The timing is critical—do the texturing too soon, and the vinegar paint flows back over the designs, do it too late, and the paint is too hard to mark. Our best advice, in light of our first sticky mistakes, is to cut yourself a stack of scrap wood tiles, and to run a series of color and time trials.

CHOOSING THE PAINTS, COLORS, MATERIALS, AND BRUSHES

Keep in mind that although we say to use such and such a color and mix to decorate a small box, this is not to say that you should unhesitatingly follow our directions. We may like cool colors for the ground coats, but there's no reason why you can't go for other traditional colors like bright chrome-yellow, earth red, or whatever.

You need a flat color for the base coat, a mix of clear varnish, brown vinegar, artist's oil-based color and mineral/white spirit for the glaze, a household brush to suit the size of your chosen item, and a metal/plastic graining comb.

MATERIALS

You will need—

• a small item to decorate—we have chosen a small steam-bent box
• a pack of graded sandpapers
• a quantity of flat vinyl/latex paint in a soft color, like yellow ochre
• a can of clear varnish
• a tube of raw umber, artist's quality oil-based paint
• a quantity of brown malt vinegar
• a quantity of mineral/white spirit

4-2   Work the brush in the direction of the grain. Note how the separation of the vinegar and oil mix creates its own characteristic texture/pattern.

• a metal/plastic graining comb
• all the usual around-the-house items like newspapers, running water, old cloths, and various spoons for mixing

PROJECT STAGES

Preparation
Take your selected item—new or found—and check it over just to make sure that it's in good, sound clean condition. For example, with our new box, since the lap-over of thin wood that goes to make the lid of the box was coming apart, it needed to be reglued and clamped. Remove loose paint, grease, dust, or whatever.

Take the graded sandpapers, and working through the grades from rough to fine, sand the surface to a smooth finish. This done, give the surface to be decorated a coat of thin varnish to seal the wood, and let it dry. Finally, when the varnish is completely dry, use a fine-grade sandpaper to rub down the whiskers and nibs of grain.

Laying On the Ground
When you are happy with the piece, give it an all-over coat of the flat vinyl/latex paint, and put it to one side to dry. Sand back to a smooth finish, and lay on another coat of paint. Repeat this procedure three or

four times until the surface is flat and silky smooth. Pay particular attention to the bottom edge of the box, and the edges of the lid.

Working the Design

Once the ground paint is dry, then you can start the exciting—if slightly sticky and smelly—task of vinegar painting.

Decant about a ¼ cup of varnish into a throwaway container. Add a generous worm of umber artist's quality oil-based paint to the varnish, plus a splash or two of mineral/white spirit, and stir the mix together until the oil paint is completely blended in. You should finish up with a slightly thin, golden-brown varnish glaze.

Now for the easy bit. Add about one egg cup of brown vinegar to the glaze, and whisk rapidly with a stick or an old fork. Continue until the mix becomes an emulsion—like vinegar-and-oil salad dressing. That is to say, the water-based vinegar and the oil-based varnish will seem to be blended together, but in fact the two components will be wanting to separate.

As soon as you achieve the vinegar mix, give the flat painted surface a generous coat, and then clear the decks ready for action. It might be just as well to also paint a small test piece.

After a few minutes the two components of the mix will start to ''quarrel'' and separate, with the magical effect that the brown painted surface will start to ''crawl'' (see **4-2**). If all is well, the brown varnish will begin to take on a curious pattern—almost like brown wood graining. When this begins to happen, test the trial piece by making a mark with the point of a compass or other tool.

When the vinegar varnish reaches a stage where the marks stay put, then you can start the combing. The combing is very straightforward; all you do is run the comb over the surface—this way and that—making patterns. You will soon get to see that each stroke makes its own characteristic mark (see **4-3**).

4-3 Working drawing—the scale is four grid squares to 1". We used three simple strokes—a fan pivot, a wavy stroke, and a whiplash flourish.

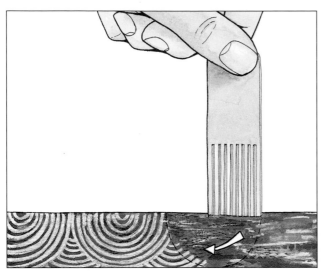

4-4 *To create the fan design pivot the comb to make a half-circle shape.*

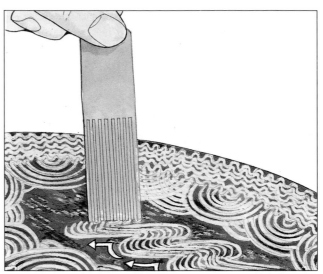

4-6 *Make a swift, wavy on-off dash at the middle of the lid to create the whiplash pattern.*

Take the comb and, working around the sides of the box, pivot the comb to make the fan shapes (see **4-4**). Next, working on the lid, comb around the edge to make a continuous wavy ribbon design to create a frame around the oval shape (see **4-5**). Last, make a whiplash flourish in the middle (see **4-6**).

Special Tip There are literally hundreds of viable pattern combinations. And, of course, you can make marks with just about anything that takes your fancy—a hair comb, a stiff bristle brush, a corn cob, a screw of stiff paper, your fingers—there are any number of possibilities.

Finishing

When you are happy with the overall effect, clean up and wait until the combed surface is completely dry. Finally, sign and date the base, give the whole works a thin coat of clear varnish, and the project is complete.

AFTERTHOUGHTS

• There are any number of exciting color and texture possibilities—you could tint the varnish with red oil-based paint rather than umber, you could lay the mix over a striped red-and-yellow base, you could go for a crumpled texture rather than combing, you could try a different proportion of vinegar, and so on.
• Some plastic throwaway containers break down when they come into contact with varnish and spirit. They wrinkle, sag, and leak. With this in mind, either use glass jars or cans or make certain that you never leave your mix in suspect containers.
• The old-timers used found natural items to texture the vinegar-varnished finish—corn husks and cobs, leaves, feathers, fir cones, and such.

4-5 *Comb the little wavy curl-like border around the edge of the lid.*

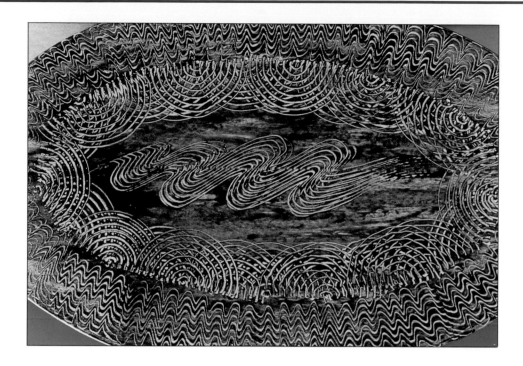

• Graining combs come in all shapes and sizes—old ones are made from metal and leather, but you can now get ones made from plastic. We got ours from a house decorator's shop.

• As our box was new and steam-bent, there was a tendency for the grain to shell off as long splinters. The varnish helps to seal and stabilize the surface and hold down the grain.

• If you do decide to run a series of time and technique trials, make sure that you label each sample so that you have a record for next time around. You will be happy you did.

—5—
Candle Marbling

CANDLE MARBLING, SOMETIMES referred to by the old-timers as smoke marbling, or even simply as marbling, is one of those magical techniques that characterizes Pennsylvania painting (see **5-1**). For us the technique somehow encapsulates the times and conditions in which the painters worked.

Its well worth remembering that the early Pennsylvania painters—usually itinerants, but often talented members of the household—didn't have access to books on decoration, nor were they working in an environment where they could readily ask a coworker or friend how such and such a technique worked. For the most part, they were working on their own, under primitive conditions, using simple homemade tools and raw materials that they gleaned from the area in which they worked.

5-1   Project picture.

Candle marbling must surely have been one of those techniques that was discovered by chance. Perhaps, a journeyman painter working by candlelight at the end of a long day, ready for payment of cash and supper, has just varnished a small box, and is giving it one last lookover. Picking up the box to inspect his handiwork, he holds it close to the candlelight, and before he knows it, the carbon from the candle marks the tacky varnish. He can't do much other than come back to it when the varnish is dry. When he returns, he finds that the candle carbon has permanently colored and stained the varnish. But then again, he also notes that the smoked effect is a bit like marble, and really quite beautiful. Possibilities come to mind.

Apart from these fanciful imaginings, candle marbling is a delightfully easy and "instant" technique. The interesting thing is that the black smoky trails and wisps given off by the candle are somehow taken up and captured by the varnish. The feel of the shiny varnish surface is unchanged—still smooth and glossy—but the smoked areas range in color from deep inky black to smoky grey.

Having said that the technique is easy, we must add the proviso that you do have to get all the conditions just right. For example, if you hold the candle too close, the surface will blister; if you don't hold it close enough, the candle will refuse to smoke; if you do it when the varnish has passed the tacky stage, the carbon will wipe off. And, of course, most important of all you must always be mindful that exposed flames and wet varnish are not a happy mix. Best not to say too much about my first attempt at smoke marbling—the flame flash was amazing and I can still smell the singed hair—other than to say that you must wait until

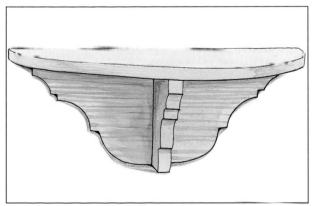

5-2 The green-painted shelf ready for marbling.

the varnish is almost dry, you must work well away from opened cans of varnish and mineral spirit, and on no account should you work in a small enclosed space.

CHOOSING THE PAINTS, COLORS, MATERIALS, AND BRUSHES

In terms of paints and materials, this project couldn't be easier. All you require is a flat vinyl/latex paint for the ground, a clear varnish for the finish, and, of course, a lighted candle.

As for brushes, a single ½″ household brush will do just fine.

MATERIALS

You will need—

• a small easy-to-hold piece to decorate. We have used a small console shelf, but you could just as well go for something like a box, or small stool, or maybe a small piece of furniture like a chair
• a pack of graded sandpapers
• a quantity of flat vinyl/latex paint in a soft yellow-green color
• a can of clear varnish
• a quantity of mineral/white spirit for cleaning the brush
• a pack of white domestic candles
• all the usual around-the-house items like newspapers, running water, old cloths, and various spoons for mixing

PROJECT STAGES

Preparation

When we say that you can decorate just about any small piece of woodware—anything from a little shelf (see 5-2) to a chair—our thinking has to do with the supposition that traditionally the technique involved the lone painter holding the item in one hand and the candle in the other. That said, it occurs to us that, given enough help and/or time, you could in fact decorate quite a large piece of furniture. So, for example, let's say that you wanted to smoke a chest. You could varnish one side, hang it from ropes or whatever, and then do the smoking on the underside. Certainly it would take days rather than hours to smoke all the sides, but it could be done.

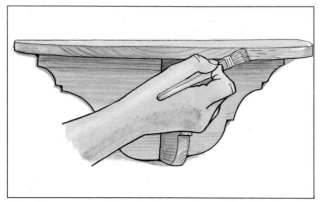

5-3 Lay on a well-brushed coat of varnish—brush out runs and dribbles.

Take your selected item, and spend time preparing the surface that is to be decorated. Set nails below the surface, fill holes and splits, and generally tidy it up. Or, as the old-time accounts say, ''Bring to order and make good.'' This done, sand to a good smooth finish, and wipe with a damp cloth.

Spend time setting out your tools and arranging the working area. Make sure that the actual smoking can be done well away from combustibles. If necessary, plan the project so that the smoking can be done out of doors.

Laying On the Ground

Being pleased with the preparation, take the yellow-green flat vinyl/latex paint, and give the item a single well-brushed coat. Wait for the paint to dry, and then repeat the procedure three or four times until you achieve a super-smooth finish. Don't forget that the final finish relies, to a great extent, on the ground being as smooth as possible (see **5-2**).

Working the Design

Wait until the water-based ground coat is completely dry, then give the workpiece a swift but well-brushed coat of varnish to cover. Be generous with the varnish, but not so generous that there are lots of dribbles (see **5-3**).

Now for the fun bit! Having waited for the varnish to dry to the tacky stage, light the candle, and get to work. With the workpiece held in one hand and the candle in the other, play the smoky bit at the peak of the candle flame over the varnished surface (see **5-4**). You will soon see that the angle of the surface to the flame and the closeness of the flame are all factors that go to creating the character of the marbling. For example, if the candle is at right angles to the surface, it produces a round smoky shape; if the surface is held so that the smoke can hit it and then drift upwards, it

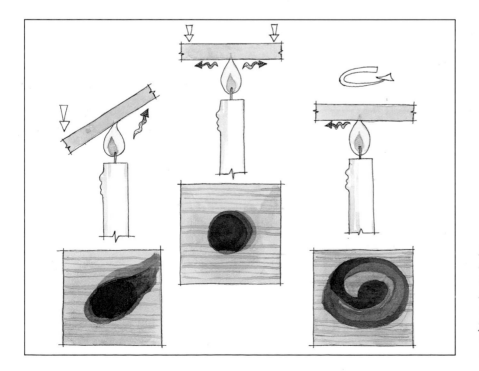

5-4 (Left) Holding the surface at an angle to the flame creates an oval shape. (Middle) Holding the surface directly above the flame makes a circle shape. (Right) If you slowly move the surface and/or the flame, you will create a trailed effect.

5-5 *The varnish takes up the candle carbon to make a permanent coloration.*

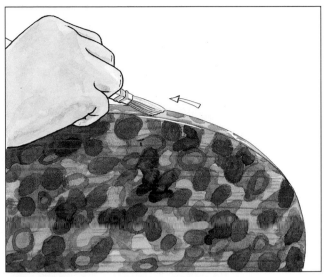

5-6 *When you are finished with the candle, and the first coat of varnish is dry, then lay on another thin coat to cover.*

produces a pear-shaped streak (see **5-5**); and then yet again, if you swirl the candle you produce a smoky whorl, and so on.

Special Tip If you have the time and the inclination, you could cut a number of plywood tiles, paint them in different flat colors, and run a series of trials. You could experiment with various angles and movements. Don't forget to write the paint type and directions you followed on the back of the trials.

And so you continue, variously playing the candle flame over the varnished surface until you have achieved what you consider is a good pattern. Repeat this procedure for all surfaces that you want to decorate.

Finishing
There is really not much to say about the finishing other than, if you want to go for a super-smooth finish, then the more coats of varnish you lay down over the smoked coat, the better (see **5-6** and **5-7**).

If by chance the smoked varnish blisters, rub the blisters down with the fine-grade sandpaper, and lay on extra coats of varnish.

5-7 *(From left to right) When you are varnishing, always start with the edges. Work in the direction of the grain. Use a soft, stroking action, all the while watching out for runs. Work from the middle to the sides, and finish up with a single through-stroke.*

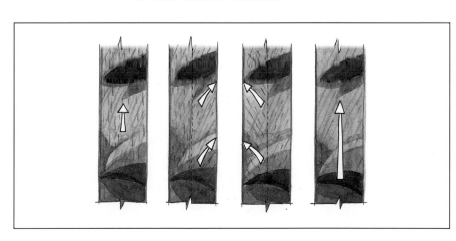

AFTERTHOUGHTS

• If you are a "nervous" beginner, then wear gloves, a nonflammable visor, and work outside.

• Since the trick is judging precisely when the varnish is ready, you might run a series of test pieces alongside the project. When such and such a test piece is ready, then it follows that you can start on the workpiece.

• Traditionally, the Pennsylvania painters were very fond of smoking over an off-white base coat to produce a white-marble effect.

• In the interests of safety, *never* leave spirit-soaked rags in the house, have a helper watch over you while you work, have your hair tied back if it is long, and make sure that you are ready for a fire, with an extinguisher/fire blanket.

—6—
Pennsylvania Barn Hex Stool

HAVE A LOOK at the project picture (see **6-1**), the design grid (see **6-2**), and the working drawings (see **6-3**). Notice how, although we have used the barn hex motif to decorate the top of a small, three-legged, round-top stool, we could just as well have used it to decorate a box, table, cupboard door, or the garden shed.

The pleasure of this project, it seems to us, lies not so much in the context of the decoration, but rather in the way the hex is drawn out and painted.

Although some authorities maintain that the Pennsylvania Germans more or less "invented" the hex motif, we think it must be pointed out that similar motifs—meaning six-pointed stars contained within a circle—can be found in medieval cathedrals in the form of windows and tracery, on old English carved chests as chip-carved motifs, on old German fraktur manuscripts, and so on. That said, we consider that the Pennsylvania Germans certainly scored a "first" when they came up with the incredible idea of decorating barns with painted hex-stars at six feet across.

6-1   Project picture—the finished hex design.

As to the old belief that hex-stars possessed magical qualities, for us the magic lies in the rather mysterious truth that they can be drawn with nothing more complicated than a compass, a straightedge, and a pencil.

If you have a look at our working drawings (see **6-3**), you will see that drawing the hex circle is pretty straightforward. And, of course, if you can use the procedure to draw six-pointed stars, then it follows that you can just as easily use it to draw out stars with 12 points, 24 points, and so forth. We must point out that although the technique is fine for drawing out large, simple forms, it falls short when it comes to pure ''mathematics.'' For instance, the radius of a circle doesn't exactly step-off six times around the circumference of its circle. It's really 6.2 something times; the ratio of the circumference of a circle to its diameter—referred to a Pi—is a fundamental, ''transcendental'' number, with the approximate value 3.141592 . . .

CHOOSING THE PAINTS, COLORS, MATERIALS, AND BRUSHES

In terms of paint and tools, this project is one of the easiest in the book in that it uses nothing more complicated than green milk paint, flat acrylic paint, a tinted varnish glaze, beeswax polish, and a couple of soft-haired, sable brushes.

MATERIALS

You will need—

• a small piece of furniture to decorate—our stool has a top about 10″ in diameter
• a pair of large fixed-leg compasses
• a pack of graded sandpapers
• a quantity of flat vinyl/latex paint in a soft yellow-green color
• acrylic paints in the colors yellow, red, and white
• a couple of soft-haired, sable watercolor brushes—a broad- and a fine-point
• a can of clear varnish
• a quantity of mineral/white spirit for thinning the varnish
• a tube of umber artist's quality oil color
• a collection of throwaway cans and jars
• all the usual around-the-house items like newspapers, running water, old cloths, and various spoons for mixing and stirring

PROJECT STAGES

Preparation

It's probably best if we simply describe how we prepared our stool, and then you can modify the techniques to suit your selected piece. We found our stool literally in the attic of our house. It was painted a bright flat orange. All we did was give it a wash in tepid soapy water and sand it down with fine-grade sandpaper, and the task was done.

Having selected your piece, first check it over, just to make sure that it's sound, and then sand it with the graded sandpaper. Don't bother to strip the surface back to the wood, simply clean off the loose paint, make certain that the surface is stable, and sand to a smooth finish.

Laying On the Ground

When you have achieved a relatively smooth stable finish—meaning a surface that isn't going to react, flake, or in any way misbehave—then set your piece at a good working height, and spend time stirring the paints, placing all your dishes and cloths to that they are close at hand, and generally making ready.

To mix the green ground color, add water to ¼ cup of nonfat milk powder, and stir until you have a thick syrup. Add the green vinyl/latex paint little by little to the syrup—until you have about one cup—and then stir the total mix until all of the ingredients are nicely blended together.

When you have had a tryout with the paint and are happy with the texture and color, lay on a single all-over coat, and let it dry. This done, give the whole works a quick sanding with the finest-grade sandpaper, and then lay on another thin coat.

Last, when both coats are completely dry, repeat the sanding until you have cut through the paint at edges and corners.

Special Tip If you look very closely at our illustrations, you will see how, by sanding around the top edge of the seat slab, we have revealed the color of the underlying paint and wood, with the effect that we have emphasized the turned shape of the edge of the slab. Or to put it another way, by sanding through the paint at the edge, we have created lines that draw attention to the rather delicate moulding at the edge of the seat slab.

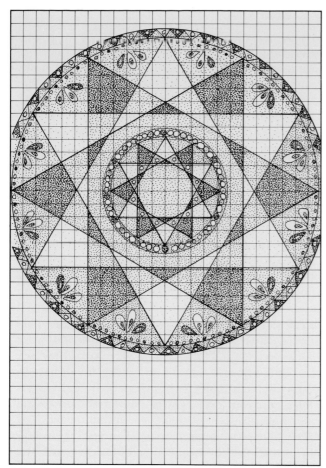

6-2 *Design grid—the scale is approximately two grid squares to 1".*

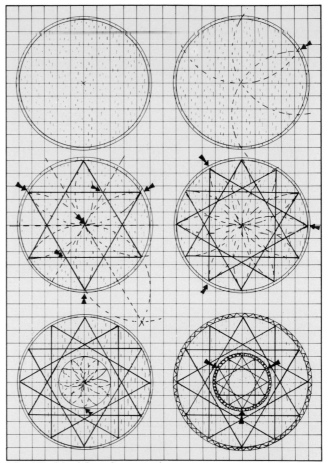

6-3 *Working drawing—setting-out stages. (Top left) Draw out the circle. (Top right) Scribe out the radius arcs. (Middle left) Link up the arc/circumference intersections for the primary star. (Middle right) Link up the arc/circumference intersections for the secondary star. (Bottom left) Draw out the hex-star at the center. (Bottom right) Complete the fancy details.*

Setting Out the Design

Decide by eye just how big you want your circle to be, set the compass to the desired radius, and fix the screw so that the legs stay put.

Spike the compass down on the center point, and draw a good, clean circle (see **6-3**, top left). Next, spike the compass on the circle—at any point around the circumference—and then step-off around the drawn line, until you reach the starting point. You should have made six marks (see **6-3**, top right).

Using the pencil and ruler, carefully draw straight lines to link every other mark. If all is well, you should have two large triangles, which in turn go to make a six-pointed star (see **6-3**, middle left).

Take the pencil and straightedge, and carefully draw straight lines that pass through the angles—meaning the "valleys" between the points of the star—and the center of the circle. Do this three times to create six step-offs that mark the halfway position between neighboring star points.

With the six marks in place, repeat the drawing procedure to draw a second six-pointed star over the first so that you have, in effect, a star with twelve points (see **6-3**, middle right).

When you have drawn the large twelve-pointed star, as illustrated, draw a smaller circle at the center of the star, and then repeat the entire procedure until you have a smaller twelve-pointed star set at the center of the first (see **6-3**, bottom).

Special Tip By following and then repeating the procedure as described, it is possible to draw a star within a star within a star, and so on, ad infinitum. We once saw a whole dance hall floor set out in this way. How about decorating your hall or foyer floor?

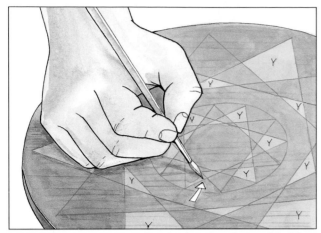

6-4   Use a fine brush to line in the edges before blocking in.

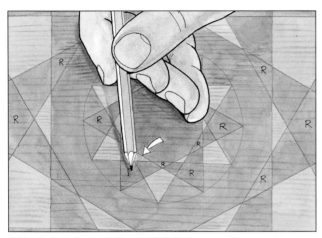

6-5   Label the red shapes lightly in pencil to avoid any confusion.

6-6   Use the fine-point brush to paint in the jewel-like details.

Painting the Design

Have a look at our design grid (see **6-2**) and other illustrations to see how the project hinges on the shapes—meaning the various rings that go to make up the design—being painted alternately red and yellow. So, for example, the twelve outer points are painted in the sequence red, yellow, red, yellow . . . and then the next ring in is painted so that there is a color transposition. This sequence is repeated all the way through to the center of the circle so that neighboring colors are always different. Or to put it another way, there is never an instant where two blocks of the same color are adjacent.

When you have a clear understanding of how the color sequence runs, take a soft pencil, and label the various triangles and diamonds so that there is no doubt what color goes where. Having carefully stirred the colors so that they are of a heavy, nonrunny consistency, take a small fine-point sable brush, and work around the design, blocking in the areas of yellow (see **6-4**). Being mindful that the success of the design relies on the color blocks being cleanly and crisply painted, do your very best to paint right up to the drawn line, so that the forms are straightedged. Lay on several thickly textured coats. Wait until the yellow paint is dry, and then repeat the procedure with the red blocks (see **6-5**).

Having filled in all the blocks of color, and waited for the paint to dry, then take a smaller brush, and color in the little triangles that run around the outer edge of the circle. Next, dab three "petals" of color—red, white, and yellow—on the areas of green that occur between each of the outermost star points. Note that we have also painted the decorative leg turnings.

Finally, use a fine-point brush to dot the red, white and yellow "jewels" of color around the design (see **6-6**).

Finishing

Having cleared away all your paints, washed the brushes under running water, and waited for the colors to dry, then comes the task of mixing the varnish glaze.

Decant a small amount of clear varnish, add a small "worm" of artist's umber oil-based color, and a dash of mineral/white spirit to the mix, and gently stir the three ingredients together. Have a tryout. If all is well, you should finish up with a delicately tinted orange-brown glaze.

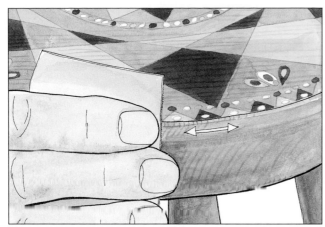

6-7   Use the fine-grade sandpaper to create "wear" areas.

6-8   Use a small pad to work the wax polish into the brush-textured surface—use a tight, circular action.

Special Tip The more artist's oil-based paint you add to the varnish, the slower the drying time. Certainly you could add two little worms rather than one, but no more. It's best to achieve a darker tint by laying on repeated coats of a light glaze.

Lay on one or more coats of varnish glaze to suit, and put the project to one side until the glaze is completely dry. If all is well—with the yellow and red painted areas being heavily textured—there will be a slight buildup of glaze in the "dips," with the effect that the glaze looks to be dappled.

Take your finest grade of sandpaper and sand the whole face of the work to cut through the glaze to reveal the "peaks" of underlying color (see **6-7**). The overall effect should be of an old painted surface that has been well worn and polished over many years—lots of dust and a buildup of wax.

Finally, wipe away the sanding dust, give the whole stool a coat of wax polish, burnish it to a dull sheen, and the project is finished (see **6-8**).

AFTERTHOUGHTS

• If you are a beginner—and bearing in mind the success of this project hinges on the hex-star being carefully drawn—it might be just as well to spend time, prior to the project, playing with a compass, and drawing out hex-stars.

• The acrylic paint needs to be thick enough to leave a heavy texture. If, when you open your jar of paint, there is a layer of liquid on the top, pour if off, stir up the paint, and then slowly return the decanted liquid until the paint is the correct consistency.

• In many ways the success of this project—and all of the projects in the book—rely on your choice of color. If, for example, you use modern colors like lime green, or dayglow pink, then no matter how well you work the techniques, the projects will look raw and out of time. You can't go wrong with earth colors and basic primaries.

—7—
Tulip Dower Chest

HAVE A LOOK at the project picture (see **7-1**) and the working drawings (see **7-2**), and see how our painted imagery draws its inspiration from traditional eighteenth-century Pennsylvania dower chests. That is to say, the overall design contains a good number of characteristic motifs—stylized tulips, a tree-of-life vine, a vase, corner hearts, zigzag borders, and dotted highlights.

The painting method, or style, is particularly exciting and dynamic in that the layout and theme allow for a considerable amount of spontaneous improvisation. This is not to say that it steps outside the Pennsylvania tradition, but rather that selected areas can be modified easily and filled in by extending forms and making motif repeats.

If you look at the front panel, you will see that although we have achieved a symmetrical layout by having three large tulip motifs, we could just as well have gone for five, or seven. That said, the Pennsylvania painters were very fond of triptych design themes—three panels, three motifs, dividing each side into three main areas of interest, and so forth.

7-1 Project picture.

64

7-2 *Design grid—the scale is three grid squares to 1". (Top) The lid design—up to the centerline. (Bottom) Front design—up to the centerline.*

Having decided to stay with the three motifs, it was a bit of a problem, because the proportions of our chest were somewhat different from the originals. When we came to finalizing the layout and design in the context of our chosen chest, we came to the conclusion that the best way of achieving a good fit and balance was to increase the size of the motifs and then stretch them to be slightly wider.

Although our design uses colors and forms that many traditionalists would no doubt consider a bit wild, there's no denying that the uninhibited joyfulness of the finished chest and the lavish use of color and brush stroke bear witness to our modest achievement of having remained true to the spirit of the old-time Pennsylvania painters.

Finally, note how we have used very basic and naive techniques—a thin milk wash for the ground, simple brushwork for the design details, a quick sanding with fine-grade sandpaper, and a thin, tinted varnish glaze for the finish.

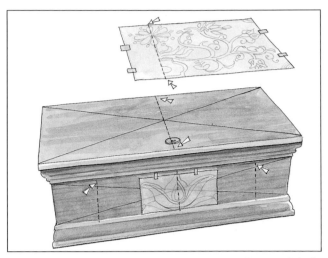

7-3   Align the traced design with the centerline, and fix it in place with tabs of masking tape.

7-4   Paint all of the green lines, the central flower stamens, the stems, and the leaves.

CHOOSING THE PAINTS, COLORS, MATERIALS, AND BRUSHES

This project uses three primary paint types: a homemade milk paint colorwash for the ground, a mixture of milk paint and acrylics for the details, and a thin, homemade varnish glaze for the finish.

We use ordinary household brushes for both the ground and the finish, and soft-haired, sable watercolor brushes for the details.

MATERIALS

You will need—

• a chest to decorate—ours stands 33″ long, 16″ wide, and 12½″ high from the base to the top of the lid
• a large sheet of workout and tracing paper to fit the various sides of your chosen chest
• a pack of graded sandpapers
• a can/pack of instant dried nonfat milk powder
• acrylic paints in the colors green, red, black, blue, yellow, and white
• a couple of inexpensive household paintbrushes about ½″ and 1″ wide
• a can of clear varnish
• a quantity of mineral/white spirit for thinning the varnish
• a tube of artist's quality oil-based paint in the color raw umber
• a collection of throwaway cans and jars
• all the usual around-the-house items like newspapers, running water, a pencil and ruler, old cloths, and various old spoons for mixing and stirring

PROJECT STAGES

Preparation
Take your "found" chest, make sure that it's not actually a valuable antique piece, and set to work removing the hardware. Ease out old nails and screws, remove handles, and generally clear away the clutter. If the handles are in any way interesting—say they are made of brass or maybe made of iron but nicely aged—then put them to one side for later use.

If you look very closely at our illustrations, you will see that our oval-shaped brass lock plate—smack in the middle of the vase—became an interesting design feature.

With all the hardware carefully removed, rub your hands carefully over the surface to ensure that it's free from nail heads, splinters, and such, and then wipe it with a damp cloth. Have a close-up look and make sure that the chest is in sound condition, that is to say, no rot, or soggy areas, or splits that threaten to rend the panels asunder. As needed, reglue and renail joints, and make good any large splits with either plaster and/or slivers of glued wood.

7-5 *Paint all the large red areas on the vase, flowers, and leaves.*

Last, scrape off any paint, and sand the wood to a smooth workable finish. Don't worry too much about a buildup of old paint in corners or water stains, just make sure that you have cleared away the loose paint and any oil stains.

Laying On the Ground

Once you have prepared the chest, then clear away all the debris, wipe away the dust, and move to the clean area that you have set aside for painting.

Start by setting the chest up at a good comfortable working height—maybe on trestles or on an old table.

Put a cup of instant nonfat milk powder into a large throwaway container, add cold water, and stir until you have a thick milky syrup. This done, add an egg spoon of your chosen acrylic green, and give the resultant mix a good stirring. Spend time blending all the lumps of milk and color until you have a smooth milk.

Test the paint out on a scrap of wood and let it dry. If you want to modify the color, simply add more green, or a dash of yellow or blue.

When you have achieved what you consider is a well-blended color, give the chest a single see-through coat—brushed in the direction of the grain—and put it to one side to dry. If all is well, the density of the paint should vary at edges and mouldings, so that the overall appearance of the chest conveys the impression that the finish has faded. If you have any leftover paint, store it in a screw-top jar.

Having waited until the paint is completely dry, take a sheet of fine-grade sandpaper and cut through at "wear" areas—on corners and sharp edges.

Setting Out the Design

Take a pencil and straightedge, and establish the center point of the sides and lid by drawing crossed diagonals. Having studied our design and maybe made modifications, use either the grid method or a photocopy machine to bring the design to size. Not forgetting that opposite sides are more or less identical, you need a total of two layouts, one for the sides, and one for the top of the lid.

When you have achieved full-size drawings, take a soft pencil and make good clear tracings. One side at a time, reverse the tracing so that the drawn lines are looking to the wood, align the design with the center point, and fix it in place with tabs of masking tape (see **7-3**). This is an important stage, so spend time getting it right.

With the tracings correctly aligned, take a hard pencil or a ballpoint pen, and carefully go over the drawn lines. Every now and then along the way, take a peek under the edge of the tracing, just to make sure that you are pressing hard enough.

Finally, having completed the transferring, remove the tracing, and, as needed, tidy up the transferred lines with a pencil.

Painting the Design

With all the designs in place, then comes the wonderfully exciting and joyful task of painting. This is the bit that we like best—stirring the pots of paint, setting out the jars of water, arranging the drawings and photographs so that they are within view, selecting brushes, maybe turning on a bit of soft background music—great!

Beginning with the design on the chest lid, take a medium-fine brush and the light-green color, and paint in the main lines—the stems, the tendrils, the spokes that go to make up the central flower (see **7-4**), and so on. Don't be too worried about deviating a little from the pencil guidelines, simply do your best to achieve a relaxed, clean-curved line. Next, block in the red vase, the red tulips, the large red petals, and so on (see **7-5**). And so you continue, working through the different colors, blocking in the areas that go to make up the design. When you have completed the lid, then repeat the procedures on the chest sides.

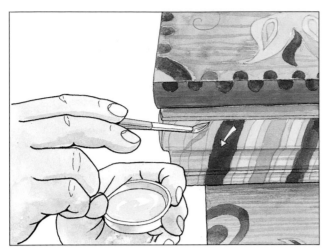

7-6   *Paint the sequence of red, yellow, and green dashes that run around the moulding.*

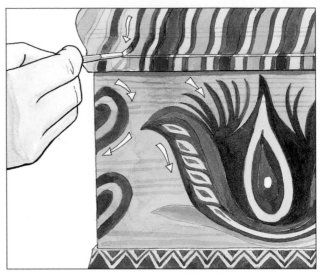

7-7   *Working with the black paint and the long-haired fine-point brush, set to work carefully edge-lining the design.*

While the colors are at hand, paint the red, yellow, green sequence of dashes around the rim moulding—meaning the decorative moulding that runs around the rim and just below the lid—the zigzag around the sides, the alternate dabs of color around the edge of the lid, and so forth (see **7-6**).

With all the main blocks of color in place, and having waited for the paint to dry, take the black paint and a long-haired, fine-point sable brush, and set to work edge-lining the design. Don't worry too much if your brush wanders, or if you have a sudden urge to paint in another feature, just go at it with vigor and enthusiasm (see **7-7**).

Special Tip If you really do have the desire to paint in dates, initials, love hearts, messages to your partner, poems, or just about anything else that takes your fancy, then our advice is to go ahead and do it.

When you are happy with the overall arrangement of colors and black-lining, take a small brush and some thick nonrunny white paint, and dot in the lines of white spots that go to make the decorative "jewel" edging (see **7-8**). Work around the whole design, all the while aiming to keep the dots about ⅛″ to ¼″ away from each other and from the black lines. And so you continue, brushing in more color, adjusting the black lines, maybe filling a space with another motif, all the while working backwards and forward, and over and around the chest, until the whole works is a riot of color and pattern—and until you are pleased.

Finishing

When everything is dry, take what remains of your green milk paint, thin it down slightly, add the small dab of white, and then give the whole chest another wash (see **7-9**). When the wash is dry, use fine-grade sandpaper to sand through the surface at wear areas (see **7-10**).

7-8   *Use the fine-point brush and the white paint to pick out the pearl-like dots that enrich the design.*

7-9   Lay on the green wash, let it dry, and finish with the golden brown glaze.

7-10   Use a fine-grade sandpaper to sand through the wash and/or glaze.

Decant some of your varnish into another container, add a small dab of artist's umber oil-based color, and a dash of mineral/white spirit. Being very careful not to introduce too much air, gently stir the ingredients until you have medium varnish glaze—not runny, just a slightly tinted varnish.

Finally brush the glaze over the whole chest, screw the hardware back in place, and the job is done.

AFTERTHOUGHTS

• If your found chest is a mess to start with, and you just haven't the time and energy to sand it down, you could give it an undercoat of flat beige-colored paint, before laying on the green milk-paint wash.

• If you like the overall project, but don't much like the idea of starting with a muted green ground, then consider having a strong, bold base color like dark blue, deep brick red, or dark green.

• In the context of Pennsylvania painting, this project is very loose and free. If you like the overall design, but want to tighten it up, then first look to the other projects for inspiration; also, spend time reworking each and every motif so that they are crisply symmetrical. For example, if you look at the large tulip motifs on the front panels, you will see that although overall they are symmetrical, they are in fact very loosely drawn. You could set each tulip out with a centerline, and spend time making sure that each and every curve and detail is perfectly balanced.

• If your chosen chest is a real monster—let's say that it has been painted a nasty 60s pink, or it has been covered in fun fur and glue, or some such—then it might be a good idea to take it to a specialist, and have it dipped and stripped.

• When you are transferring symmetrical designs—as in this project—you can cut out the tedious tasks of reworking the back of the tracings simply by turning the tracing around so that the drawn lines are looking to the surface to be decorated. If the design is primarily symmetrical, but has a few nonsymmetrical details, like dates and/or initials, then trace and transfer such details separately.

—8—
Mantango Valley
Birds and Flowers Dresser

The Mantango Valley Pennsylvania Germans specialized in producing highly stylized, brilliantly painted designs on a flat colored ground. A group of eighteen or so painter-craftsmen—now sometimes referred to as the Mantango school or the Schwaben Creek school—they excelled in painting traditional motifs that were, to a greater or lesser extent, inspired by contemporary European marquetry work and fraktur designs.

If you look at our project picture (see **8-1**) and design grid (see **8-2**), you will see that the four primary motifs—the corner fan, the bird, the rosette, and the flower—are very much like motifs that occur on seventeenth- and eighteenth-century European furniture and in fraktur manuscript illustration.

8-1   Project picture.

This project draws its inspiration from one particular Mantango piece, namely, a slant-top desk, inscribed "Jacob Maser 1834." We know from old accounts that Jacob Maser was married in 1834, so the probability is that this chest was a wedding gift or, perhaps, a piece ordered for the new home. The original is in a dark blue-green color with black, yellow, and red birds.

Although we couldn't get hold of a slant-top desk, we had the good luck to be given a small much-cut-about fragment of what was, almost certainly, a larger dresser. That apart, we were fortunate on five counts. The piece is at least a hundred years old, it is generously proportioned, it had originally been painted green, we only had to remove a dozen or so coats of gloss paint, and—best of all—it was a gift from a relation of ours!

CHOOSING THE PAINTS, COLORS, MATERIALS, AND BRUSHES

This project uses a homemade milk paint colorwash for the ground, and a mixture of milk paint and acrylics for the details. It is finished with wax.

We used ordinary household brushes for the ground, and soft-haired, sable watercolor brushes for the details.

MATERIALS

You will need—

• a found piece of old pine furniture—we have used what was left of an old dresser, but you could just as well use a farmhouse-style table with a drawer, or a chest of drawers
• a pack of graded sandpapers
• a pencil, ruler, and pair of compasses
• a can/pack of instant dried nonfat milk powder, as found in most grocery stores
• acrylic paints in the colors Brunswick green, red, black, and chrome-yellow
• a 1″ household paintbrush
• a quantity of beeswax furniture polish
• a collection of throwaway cans and jars
• all the usual around-the-house items like newspapers, running water, old cloths, and various old spoons for mixing and stirring

8-2 *Design grid—the scale is four grid squares to 1″. (Top) Large blackbird and the corner fan. (Bottom left) Design for the side panel. (Bottom right) Brush-stroke flowers for the legs.*

PROJECT STAGES

Preparation

If your found piece is anything like ours, then it will need a complete overhaul. It's best to up-end it, remove the drawer(s), check the base and the joints, and generally make sure that it's worth decorating. Scrape off paint, ease out old useless nailheads, glue and wedge shaky joints, and variously make good and bring to order. Remove any handles or catches.

When you have removed the bulk of the old paint, use the sandpaper to sand the wood to a good finish. Work through the grades from rough to smooth, all the while sanding in the direction of the grain. Finally, when you figure that the sanding is complete, close

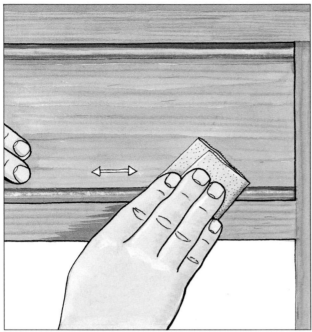

8-3   Fold the sandpaper in three, and gently sand the painted wood in the direction of the grain.

your eyes and stroke your hands over the surface—if it feels rough or you pick up splinters, then back to work!

Laying On the Ground

Add cold water to about one cup of milk powder, and stir until you have a smooth, thin syrupy mix. Add a small amount of Brunswick green to the syrup, and stir until you have a thin, runny green wash.

With your beautifully prepared piece standing before you, take a wet cloth and a small amount of red acrylic paint—just a smear—and proceed to rub the paint into the surface of the wood. Don't try to go for an ultra-tidy finish; just rub and work the paint into the grain until the wood takes on a rose-blush glow. Work all surfaces, edges, and corners.

As soon as the rubbed red paint is dry, lay on a thin coat of the green wash, let it dry slightly, and then sand the whole surface with the fine-grade sandpaper (see **8-3**). Repeat the green wash and sanding procedure three or four times. Aim for a surface that looks, on close inspection, as if it has survived many years of painting, hard wear, sanding, and repainting.

Setting Out the Design

Draw the design to size to fit your chosen piece, and make tracings. Set the surface to be decorated out with pencil guidelines, and then carefully align the tracings, fix them in place with tabs of masking tape, and pencil-press-transfer the images onto the wood (see **8-4**). And of course if your piece has two drawers, or larger panels, then modify the placing accordingly. You might repeat the birds so that you have two pairs, or you might have the tree/flower motif on the front as well as on the side, and so on (see **8-5**). When you come to the rosettes that run up the sides of the legs, simply fix the center points. And so you continue, press-transferring, establishing center points, reworking lines (see **8-6**), adding and modifying motifs to fit the space, until you are satisfied. Don't forget to establish the size of the corner fans by drawing a quarter circle with the compass.

8-4   Very carefully align the tracing with the centerline and base line, fix in place with tabs of masking tape, and press-transfer the design onto the wood.

8-5 (Left) Reverse the tracing, align it with the centerline and the other half of the design, and complete the press-transferring. (Right) Use the natural shape of the paint-loaded brush to create the petal shapes. Paint the primary "N, S, E, W" petals, and then fill in with the secondary brush strokes.

Painting the Design

Once you have set out the design, then the rest is plain sailing. Start by mixing a small amount of milk syrup with each of your acrylic colors. The best method is to decant a daub of paint, add a trickle of syrup, and then stir the two ingredients together.

To paint the bird motifs the procedure is to line in the black with a fine brush and block in, line in the red, block in, and last, line in the yellow and block in. And so you continue with all the details of the small birds and the small tree.

To paint the rosettes the procedure is: having identified the red flowers, load a small brush with red paint, and systematically make the eight brush strokes that go to make the design. Fix the size of the rosette by making strokes at north, south, east, and west (see **8-5**, bottom), and then fill in with strokes at northeast, southeast, southwest, and northwest. Paint all the red rosettes, then repeat the procedure with the yellow. Let the shape of the paint-loaded brush make its characteristic petal form.

When you come to the fans at the corners, take the red-loaded brush, start by making two lines to fix the right angle, then make three more strokes—one at the middle, and one at either side of the middle. Do this on all corners. This done, take the yellow-loaded brush, and paint a swift dash of color between the red strokes (see **8-7**).

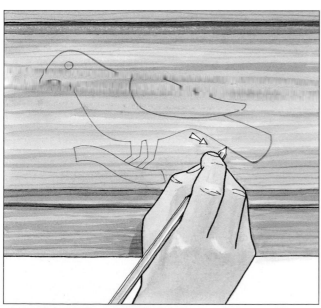

8-6 Rework the transferred images so that everything is clearly defined.

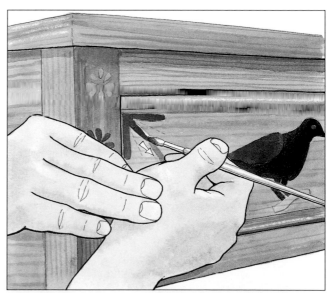

8-7 Steady and brace the brush hand to achieve confident and positive brush strokes. Do your best to avoid shaky strokes.

8-8   To achieve the ageing, use a threefold pad of fine-grade sandpaper to sand through the painted imagery. Be sure to work in the direction of the wood grain.

8-9   Use a pad of soft cloth to work the mix of fine paint dust and wax into the aged surface.

Finishing

Having taken the design as far as you want it to go, use the fine sandpaper to slightly sand through and blur the painted imagery (see **8-8**). Don't overdo this stage; just cut through the paint to break up the color. Take a soft cloth, and rub the paint dust over the whole surface to ingrain the painted images with a suggestion of the other colors. Finally, give the whole workpiece a generous coat of beeswax polish, let it soak in, and then burnish the wood to a soft-shine finish (see **8-9**).

AFTERTHOUGHTS

• When you are searching for a piece to decorate, it's best go for what we would describe as a simple country piece. If it's made of pine with lots of knots, if it has been painted dozens of times, and if it's generously proportioned, then so much the better.

• The amount of red that you need to rub into the wood prior to laying on the ground will of course depend on the age and color of your piece. If it's made of thin yellow wood, then it's going to need more color than if it's made of deep-red knotty pitch pine.

• In the context of Pennsylvania painting, only use native white woods like pine—never use exotic woods like mahogany.

• If, when you are scraping away the layers of paint, you find painted pattern, then stop work, and get the piece checked over by an expert. It wouldn't be the first time that a genuine Pennsylvania piece has been found hidden under a hundred or so years of paint!

—9—
Hearts and Tulips Door

O F ALL THE traditional motifs favored by the Pennsylvania folk artists, we think it fair to say that the tulips and the hearts are the most plentiful (see **9-1**). We've seen stylized tulip and heart motifs in fraktur drawings, on dower chests, on walls, built into hex-circle motifs, on small boxes, and in just about every decorative context that you can imagine.

9-1 Project picture—the finished door.

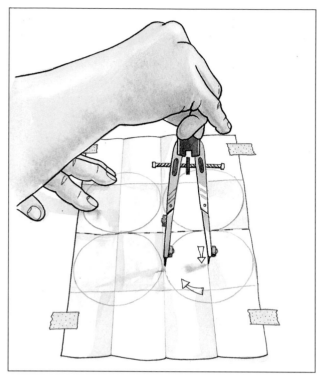

9-2   To create the characteristic heart shape use a compass to set out the four circles.

Pennsylvania tulips and hearts are unusual in that they are based on geometrical forms. If you look at our design grid (see **9-5**), you will see that the Pennsylvania hearts are not only beautifully plump in shape—quite different from, for instance, New England hearts of the same early American period—but better still they can very easily be drawn with a compass. All you do is draw four circles of the same size so that they are just touching (see **9-2**—and then link up the circumferences, as illustrated.

CHOOSING THE PAINTS, COLORS, MATERIALS, AND BRUSHES

This project is slightly different from the others in that not only do we describe how to paint the actual motifs, but more than that, we describe how to reshape and prepare the door.

We use basic tools for the simple woodwork, vinyl/latex paints for the door—the colorwash—acrylics for the motifs, and a dull-sheen varnish glaze for the finish.

MATERIALS

You will need—

• a common six-panel pine door to decorate—ours came with the house and was probably made at the turn of the century
• a sheet each of tracing and workout paper—large enough to fit your chosen door panels
• a pencil and ruler
• a general-purpose handsaw
• a pack of graded sandpapers
• a quantity of flat vinyl/latex paint in a muted blue-green color—ours was called "old Brunswick green"
• acrylic paint in a good, rich red color
• a ½" household paintbrush
• a couple of soft-haired, sable watercolor brushes—a broad- and a fine-point
• a small quantity of clear, dull-sheen varnish
• a quantity of PVA (polyvinyl acetate) wood glue
• a quantity of mineral/white spirit for thinning the varnish
• a collection of throwaway cans and jars
• all the usual around-the-house items like newspapers, running water, old cloths, and various spoons for mixing and stirring

PROJECT STAGES

Preparation

When you have chosen your door—we decided to decorate the kitchen door—take it off the hinges, and—if they are in the way—remove all the hardware. Strip away all the paint. Draw a line straight down through the center of the middle of the frame, and run it through with the saw.

Make good the cut-through joints with the glue and maybe a wedge or two of wood. When the glue is dry, use the coarse sandpaper to sand the cut edges. Next work through all the grades of sandpaper, from rough to fine, to bring the surface to a good, smooth finish.

Finally, use the fine-grade sandpaper to round over all the sharp edges.

Laying On the Ground

Having prepared the half doors, set them up on trestles, or maybe on a couple of old chairs, so that they are at a comfortable working height.

Decant about ½ cup of the green vinyl/latex paint, and top the cup off with water. Stir the mixture, and

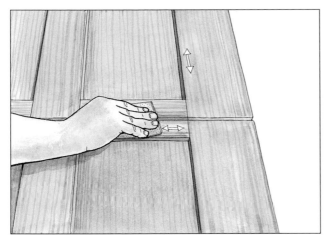

9-3 Use the fine-grade sandpaper to cut through the wash to reveal the underlying color of the wood.

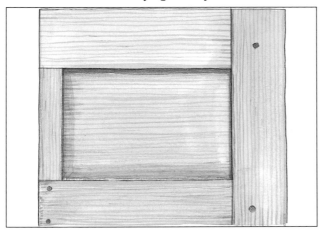

9-4 Close-up detail showing the prepared surface.

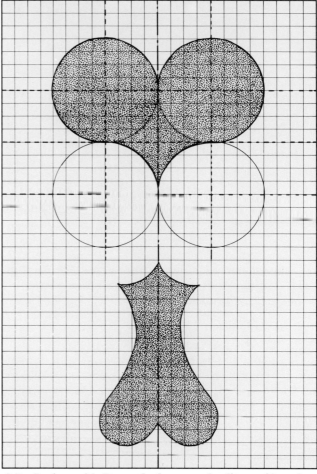

9-5 Design grid. Draw the heart and tulip motifs to fit the size of your door panels.

maybe add a drop more water, until you have a thin wash. If the mix has body, or is in any way nonrunny, then you need to add more water. The wash needs to have the color and consistency of, for example, thick, green cabbage water.

When you are happy with the mix, set to work painting the door. The best procedure is to give the door a single all-over coat, and then to lay on extra coats of color where the door would have naturally been protected from wear. So for starters, you could double up the coats around the panel edges and in the middle of the panels.

Having waited for the paint to dry, and assessed whether or not you need to lay on additional coats, take the fine-grade sandpaper, and sand the whole surface (see **9-3**). Remove all the whiskers and nibs of grain that have curled up, and generally "knock" the surface down to a smooth finish. Cut through the color at edges, at random areas within the panels, and generally blur areas that would, in the normal course of events, receive the most wear (see **9-4**).

As to how many coats of wash you apply and how many sandings you give the door, that will, of course, relate to how dark/light you want the color to be and how much you want to age the finish. At all events, the good news is that the color buildup and the sanding produce such a gradual effect that there is very little chance of making a blunder.

Setting Out the Design
Having prepared the two half doors, and studied the design grid (see **9-5**), draw the two motifs to fit the size of your panels. Make clear tracings, and mark both the tracings and the panels with centerlines.

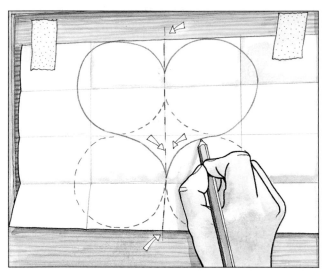

9-6   Tape the traced design in place on the door panel so that it is aligned with the centerline, and press-transfer the image onto the wood.

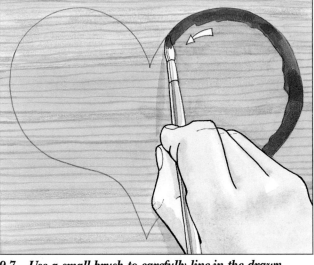

9-7 Use a small brush to carefully line-in the drawn form, and then block in. As needed, lay on a second coat to cover.

One panel at a time, align the tracings with the various guidelines—so that the pencil side is looking to the door—and press-transfer the traced lines onto the wood (see **9-6**). Make sure that all of the images are the right way up, and see to it that, from door to door, the top and bottom of the motifs are all carefully aligned.

Finally, rework the transferred lines so that there is no doubt as to the precise shape that needs to be blocked in.

Painting the Design

In many ways, by the time you get to the painting stage, the project is three-quarters finished. Take your selected acrylic color and a fine-point brush, and very carefully line in the drawn lines (see **9-7**). Work around the motif, all the while very meticulously painting to the drawn line. This done, take a larger brush and block the shape in with color. Repeat this procedure for all the motifs that go to make up the design of your chosen door. Lay on one or more coats for a dense flat cover (see **9-8**).

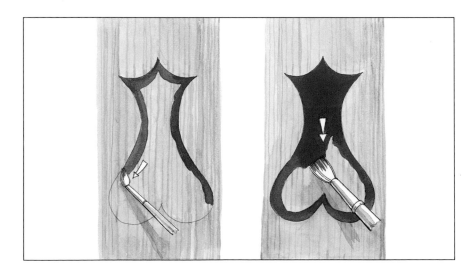

9-8   (Left) Use a fine brush to establish the outline. (Right) Use a larger brush to block in.

Finishing

Once the painted motifs are good and dry, give them a very light sanding with the finest-grade sandpaper, and clean away the dust with a soft brush or a vacuum cleaner. With the dust out of the way, and having stood back and given the whole door a last checkover just to make sure that everything is just so, lay on a couple of thin coats of dull-sheen varnish.

Study our color wash illustrations and see how we have created a homestead image by fitting our door out with a simple wooden swing bar to keep the two half doors together, a couple of handmade strap hinges, an antique iron latch, and a finger plate.

AFTERTHOUGHTS

• If you like the project, but are not so keen about the idea of cutting the door in two, then leave out that bit of the project and simply go for the decoration.

• If you want to achieve an authentic image, then you must choose the door fittings with care. Go for iron rather than brass or white metal, and have the iron rubbed down and varnished, rather than black.

• If you want to follow through and decorate a whole room in the Pennsylvania style, then it's best to visit as many museum collections as possible.

• If you want to go all the way with authenticity, you could use a milk wash for the ground, and maybe pigment and oil-based colors for the imagery.

• This project draws its inspiration from an authentic Pennsylvania six-panel door from a museum collection. If you look at our photographs, you will observe that we have done our level best to stay true to the spirit of old-time Pennsylvania painters, even to the extent that we have modified an old door, given it a color wash, and fitted it out with old hardware. If you are inclined to recreate your own authentic look-alike interior, then you are going to enjoy this project.

• It's important that you do the painting at a comfortable working height—too high and you will have neck strain, and too low and your hand will shake.

—10—
Salt Box

HAVE A LOOK at the project picture (see **10-1**) and the design grid (see **10-2**), and note that our painted imagery draws its inspiration from a design detail from a dower chest. This particular chest—signed and dated "Anne Beer, March the 18. 1790"—is somewhat atypical in than the design is particularly uninhibited. It might almost have been painted by a child. However, as the design features two mermaid nymphs—a little bit too saucy for a child's work—we expect that it was most likely painted as a one-of-a-kind by a member of the Annes family.

All our guesswork aside, it's plain to see, that the artist wasn't in any way hidebound by artistic protocol, or by a desire to slavishly follow standardized conventions.

If you have a close-up look at our design grid, and the other illustrations, you will see this project hinges primarily on the design being set out with fine-line brush strokes rather than with large blocks of color. Although most of the motifs are symmetrical, the painting style allows for a great deal of personal freedom and interpretation.

10-1 The finished box. See how we have achieved the "aged" effect by suggesting that there are other, older designs under the paint.

80

The preparation and ground painting of our salt box—a new box made from a kit—are exciting in that we have given the surfaces character by laying brushwork under the ground color, and then sanding through. The overall effect is that the box looks as if it has seen many years of daily use, repair, and repainting.

CHOOSING THE PAINTS, COLORS, MATERIALS, AND BRUSHES

This project is slightly unusual in that we have chosen to make the salt box from a kit—we prefer painting old pieces—and then, prior to painting the design, to distress the surface. The extra effort involved in preparation is offset by the final stages being very simple and direct.

We use acrylics for the under-ground colors and the designs, a milk paint for the ground, and a plain varnish finish.

MATERIALS

You will need—

• a small salt box to decorate—ours was made from a kit
• a sheet each of tracing and workout paper—large enough for all the faces of your chosen box
• a pencil and ruler
• a roll of masking tape
• a pack of graded sandpapers
• about ¼ cup of instant nonfat milk powder
• odds and ends of acrylic in such colors as yellow, red, green, and blue
• a quantity of flat vinyl/latex paint in a muted green-blue color
• acrylic paints in the colors mustard-yellow, red, and cream
• a couple of soft-haired, sable watercolor brushes—a broad- and a fine-point
• a small quantity of clear varnish
• a quantity of mineral/white spirit for thinning the varnish
• a collection of throwaway cans and jars
• all the usual around-the-house items like newspapers, running water, old cloths, and various spoons for mixing and stirring

10-2   *Design grid—the scale is four grid squares to 1".* (Top left) *Back of the box motif.* (Top right) *Side panel motif.* (Middle) *Lid motif.* (Bottom) *Front panel motif.*

PROJECT STAGES

Preparation

Having built or found your chosen salt box, start by giving it a good sanding with a medium-grade sandpaper. Sand off the sharp corners, set nails below the surface, and generally prepare the surface until it feels smooth, worn, and round-edged. Wipe away the dust, give the box a thin coat of varnish, or sealer, and let it dry.

Now for the fun bit. Bearing in mind that you are trying to duplicate years of redecoration, first give the whole box a swift all-over coat of leftover yellow, and then take your thick acrylic leftovers and set to working using the various faces of the box as a tryout for just about any other project that takes your fancy. For

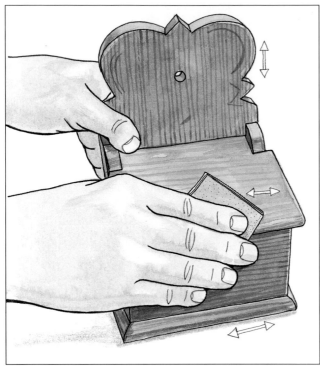

10-3   Use a fold of fine-grade sandpaper to cut through the ground paint to give a worn effect.

10-4   Align the tracing with the guidelines and press-transfer the motif onto the wood.

example, you might practise your lining techniques, practise your brush strokes, paint a message for future generations, try your hand at painting tulips, run dot-and-dash designs around the panels.

Special Tip Since the undercoat paints are, to a great extent, going to remain unseen, this is the ideal opportunity to use up odds and ends left over from other projects as well as to practise various techniques.

Laying On the Ground
Set out the milk powder, the green-blue flat vinyl/latex paint, and the box to decorate. Mix the milk powder with water until you have a thin syrupy mix, and then stir in about ½ cup of green-blue paint. Stir the mixture thoroughly, until it is smooth-running.

When you are happy with the mix—it must be free from lumps and of the right color and consistency—give the box a couple of coats, and put it to one side.

Wait until the green-blue ground is good and dry, then take your finest-graded sandpaper, and give the whole workpiece a gentle sanding (see **10-3**). Don't overdo the sanding—you might rip off the ground

paint—just go at it nice and easy until you cut through at edges and high spots. If all goes well, not only will you reveal the yellow undercoat at corners and edges, but the overall surface will be flecked with color from the underlying designs. For example, when we look closely at our box, we can see yellow breaking through on the sharp edges, little flecks and lines of red where we had a tryout at lining, small dots of bright green where we dotted a pattern, and so on. If you have done it right, the flecks of color will not only relieve the relatively large areas of flat blue, but the overall texture will fool the eye into believing that the box has age.

Setting Out the Design
When you have achieved a box with character and a past, then draw the designs to the size of the sides of the box, and make clear tracings. Establish centerlines by drawing crossed diagonals, align the tracings, and carefully press-transfer the design onto the box (see **10-4**).

Painting the Design
Having studied our imagery, stirred the paints, and generally made ready, then comes the relatively easy task of painting the designs. We say relatively, because although the design is minimal—really no more than a simple outline blocked in with color—it does have to be done with care.

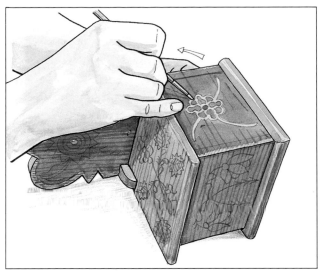

10-5 *Use your little finger to brace and steady your brush hand—also as a pivot point when painting arc/curved lines.*

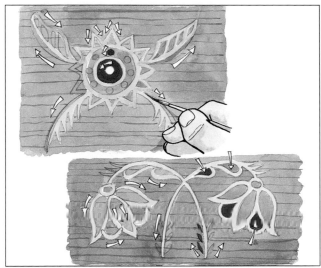

10-6 *Painting guide—showing the direction of the brush strokes, the overlapping and construction of the cream areas, and the successive overlaying of color details.*

Starting with the cream-colored outline, take a fine-point sable brush, and very carefully line in the design (see **10-5**). Work with a light, finger-supported dragging stroke. That is, load the brush with paint, wipe it to a point, set the point down on the drawn line, steady your hand by resting the little finger on the workpiece, and then draw the brush towards your body (see **10-6**). The secret lies in having a light, smooth hand

movement. And so you continue by loading the brush, wiping it to a point, and then turning the workpiece this way and that for the best angle of approach.

Use the fine brush to block in the areas of mustard-yellow (see **10-7**). Still using the fine brush, paint in the areas, make little dashes or flicks of color for the fern-like details, and the painting is finished (see **10-8**).

10-7 *Turn both the box and the brush to approach the design to best advantage.*

10-8 *To paint a detail, first use a fine brush to define the outline, and then block in.*

Finishing

Finishing couldn't be easier. Wait for the paint to dry, and then sand the whole workpiece with the finest grade of sandpaper. Once again, don't overdo the sanding, just enough to ever so slightly break through the paint.

Last, wipe away the dust with a spirit-dampened cloth, give the entire box a couple of coats of clear varnish—inside and out—and the job is done.

AFTERTHOUGHTS

• If you intend using your box for holding salt, you must remember that salt corrodes iron/steel. If you used a kit that comes complete with steel nails and pivot pins, then change the nails with brass pins, and use little pegs of wood for the pivots.

• If you want to personalize the box in the traditional Pennsylvania manner, you could build dates, names, and initials into the design.

• If you like the project, but figure to make your own box, then be sure to steer well clear of toxic woods like yew. It's best to use an uncomplicated, easy-to-work wood like pine.

• If by chance you make a mess of mixing the milk to the extent that it's full of hard lumps, then pour the mixture into a fine mesh tea strainer and sieve.

— 11 —
Transposed-Color Tulip Boxes

T HE EARLY PENNSYLVANIA homesteads were jam-packed with wooden containers of every conceivable shape and structure. There were little boxes to hang on the wall, large slatted crates for barn and shed goods, delicate baskets for carrying sewing, trays for cutlery, trinket boxes, salt boxes, boxes for books, ditty boxes, steam-bent boxes, lidded boxes for food, boxes for mixing and washing, and we could go on and on. The wonderful thing is that a good number of these containers were, to a greater or lesser degree, brightly painted.

Our two boxes draw their inspiration from a candle box that dates from about 1825. Although the original is a mass of characteristic motifs—dots, lines, curves, birds, and brush-stroke "teardrops"—the most powerful image is that of a stylized tulip in a vase. This beautifully naive motif has been repeated in transposed colors at several points around the side of the box.

11-1 *The project picture—the two finished tulip boxes.*

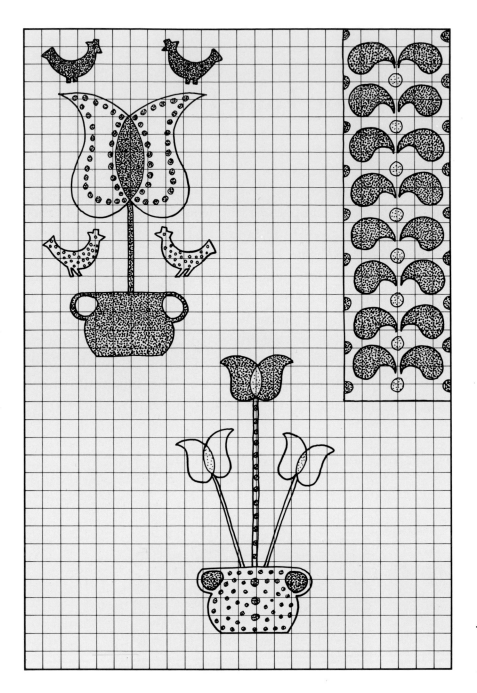

11-2 Design grid—the scale is four grid squares to 1". (Top left) Side panel design. (Top right) The corner repeat design. (Bottom) Side panel design.

From the painters' point of view, the technique of color transposition is a really good way of saving time, effort, and materials. The painters can have two colors, two brushes, and two images on the go at one and the same time. So, for example, let's say that you are working with red and yellow. You have two brushes, two pots of colors, and two tulip-vase images to decorate. You swiftly paint two vases, one yellow and one red, and then you go on, to paint a red tulip in the yellow vase, a yellow tulip in the red vase, red dots on the

yellow vase, yellow dots on the red vase, and so on. You don't need to wash brushes, or introduce new colors, you can work simply backwards and forward, all the while swapping the same brushes and colors. The great thing is, of course, that not only are you working with the minimum of effort and waste, you are also bound, in the process, to achieve a balanced design.

If you look closely at our project picture (see 11-1), you will see that having once painted the two boxes the same color, we then go on to use the transposed

86

color technique for all the motifs. The exciting illusion is that, at first sight, the imagery appears, from box to box, to be identically painted.

CHOOSING THE PAINTS, COLORS, MATERIALS, AND BRUSHES

As the project is more about the technique of color transposition rather than textures, so we have opted to use straightforward shop-bought paints. We use a domestic vinyl/latex paint for the ground color, model-makers acrylics for the imagery, and wax varnish for the finish. We use large, watercolor sable brushes for the ground, Japanese brushes for the imagery, and fine-point sables for the small details.

MATERIALS

You will need—

• two small boxes to decorate—it's best if they are more or less the same shape and size
• a sheet each of workout and tracing paper—big enough to suit your chosen boxes
• a pencil and ruler
• a pack of graded sandpapers
• a quantity of flat vinyl/latex paint in a muted yellow-ochre color
• acrylic paints in the colors red and cream
• a large soft-haired, sable watercolor brush
• two fine sable brushes
• two medium-size Japanese calligraphy brushes
• a small household brush for varnishing
• a small quantity of clear wax varnish
• a quantity of mineral/white spirit
• a collection of throwaway cans and jars
• all the usual around-the-house items like newspapers, running water, old cloths, and various spoons for mixing and stirring

PROJECT STAGES

Preparation
Once you have gathered your tools and materials, take your two boxes—new or found—and use the sandpaper to sand them to a smooth finish. As needed, remove nails, and fill cracks and holes. Having studied our design grid (see **11-2**), and seen how we use them to fill the space, draw the designs to the size of your boxes. When you are happy with the images, use a soft pencil to make tracings.

Laying On the Ground
Having decided how the boxes are going to be supported once they have been painted, wipe them over with a slightly damp cloth, and lay on a single well-brushed coat of the yellow-ochre vinyl/latex paint. When the paint is crisply dry, give the surfaces a quick sanding with the fine-grade sandpaper to remove nibs and whiskers of raised grain, and lay on one or more coats to cover. When the last coat is dry, give the surfaces to be decorated a final sanding.

Setting Out the Design
Working with a pair of small boxes of this size with images of this character, it is most important that the designs are set out with full care and attention. To this end, reverse the tracings so that the pencil side is looking at the surface to be decorated—you can do this because the designs are symmetrical—align the designs with the centerline, and secure with masking tape. Use either a hard pencil or a ballpoint pen, to press-transfer the lines of the design onto the wood (see **11-3**). Repeat this procedure with all the tracings and motifs that go to make up the total design.

11-3 Align the tracing with the guidelines, fix it in place with tabs of masking tape, and use a hard pencil to press-transfer the design onto the wood. As needed, adjust the shape, size, and complexity of the design to fit your chosen containers. For example, notice how we have left out the two top birds on the small box.

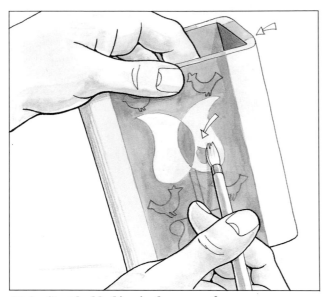

11-4   Start by blocking in the areas of cream.

11-5   Block in the areas of red.

Painting the Design

With all the guidelines in place, take the two pots of acrylic paint—red and cream—and the two Japanese brushes, and set to work. Start by blocking in the underlying areas of cream on both boxes—the vases, the large tulip center, and the small tulip petals on one, and the large tulip petals, the vases, the roosters, and corners on the other (see **11-4**). Repeat this procedure with the red paint (see **11-5**). Next use a fine sable to paint all the little decorative dot details that go to make up the design (see **11-6**). When the first blocks of color are dry, realign the corner tracings and press-transfer the stylized "teardrops" shapes onto the corners. Do this with all of the corners and on both boxes.

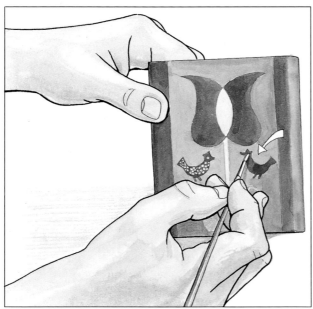

11-6   Painting the overlay color—cream on red. Use a fine brush for the small dot details.

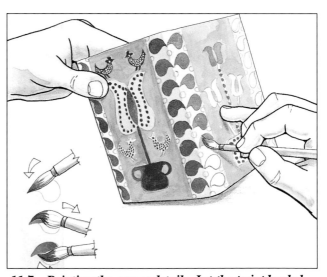

11-7   Painting the corner details. Let the paint-loaded brush make its own characteristic "teardrop" shape. First set down the tip of the brush; then, at one and the same time, turn the brush in a clockwise direction and increase the downward pressure.

When the secondary details are done, then take the Japanese brush and set to work painting red on cream, and cream on red—cream teardrop shapes on the red corners, red teardrops on the cream corners (see **11-7**). Last, paint in the small dots of the yellow-ochre base color on the corners, and the painting is finished.

Finishing

The wonderful thing about transposed color painting is the feeling that you could continue forever—dotting and dabbing, first one color and then the other, and then back to the first color and so on, ad infinitum.

When, at last, you consider that you have taken the project as far as it can go, sign and date the bottom of the boxes, and clean up the palettes and brushes. Finally, give both boxes an all-over coat of wax varnish, and the job is done.

AFTERTHOUGHTS

• When you are choosing your boxes, go for two identical, open-top containers.
• Having noted that our boxes are between 4″ and 5″ square, and being mindful that the overall size and proportion of our motifs are pretty close to the original, we recommend that you go for boxes of a similar size.
• Although all your brushes need to be looked after, Japanese brushes need extra care and attention. Wash them under running water until they are free of color, shake off excess water, shape the head, and leave to dry.
• Note that we have had to adjust the design somewhat to fit the smaller of our two boxes—we have had to leave out the top pair of birds.

—12—
Brush-Stroke Tinware Tea Caddy

PENNSYLVANIA TINWARE—COFFEE pots, mugs, candle holders, jugs, tea trays, and all manner of small vessels—was in essence created by rolling iron into thin sheets, coating the sheets with tin, variously cutting, rolling, wrapping, folding, and soldering the resultant tinplate, and then finally painting the small containers with decorative brushwork.

Made traditionally by whitesmiths—rather than by blacksmiths, who worked in black iron—Pennsylvania tin is particularly interesting in that it was often made, decorated, and marketed by family groups. So, for example, in an early Pennsylvania tinplate shop—say around 1800—the father and son might do the scribing, cutting, and soldering, the wife and daughters would, perhaps, be responsible for the painting, and another son might send the wares to peddlers.

Once made, the wares were loaded onto wagons and peddled thousands of miles across America. At one time, the painted tinwares were so common and popular that they were known simply as "Pennsylvania tin."

12-1 *Project picture—the finished tea caddy.*

12-2 *Design grid—the scale is four grid squares to 1″. (Top left) First stage—the main flower blocked in. (Top right) Adding the leaves and side flowers. (Bottom left) The final details—the black lines and the berries. (Bottom right) The lid motif—the brush-stroke petals, and the running repeat design.*

Our use of a found tea caddy (see **12-1**)—given away as a free offer—is particularly apt in that old accounts describe Pennsylvania tinwares as being so plentiful and inexpensive that they were also given away with fancy coffee, tea, and sugar. It's a great idea—buy a pound of coffee, and get it packaged in a hand-painted Pennsylvania tea caddy!

The techniques are wonderfully simple and direct, really no more than laying on a dark base coat, picking out the design with a pattern of brush strokes, and then varnishing.

CHOOSING THE PAINTS, COLORS, MATERIALS, AND BRUSHES

Although this project has to do with painting tin rather than wood, the use of the brushes and paints is much the same. We used a vinyl/latex and black ink mix for the base coat, vinyl/latex paint for the secondary ground—the circle—acrylic for most of the details, a mix of gouache and PVA (polyvinyl acetate) wood glue for the rich ochre color, and a clear varnish to finish.

91

We used large, sable watercolor brushes for the ground, and Japanese brushes and fine-point sables for the details.

MATERIALS

You will need—

• a small item of tinware—we have used a nicely made tin caddy, but you could just as well use a cake tin, a cigar tin, or almost any easy-to-find, small-size grocery tin
• a sheet of workout paper
• a pencil and ruler
• a pair of small fixed-leg compasses
• a pack of graded sandpapers
• a quantity of flat vinyl/latex paint in the colors muted blue and cream
• a small quantity of water-based black India ink—we used our drawing ink
• acrylic paints in the colors red, pale leaf-green, light leaf-green, and black
• gouache paint in the color ochre
• a small quantity of white PVA (polyvinyl acetate) wood glue
• a large soft-haired, sable watercolor brush
• a medium-size Japanese calligraphy brush
• a small fine-point sable brush
• a small household brush for varnishing
• a quantity of best-quality clear, high-shine varnish
• a quantity of mineral/white spirit
• a collection of throwaway cans and jars
• all the usual around-the-house items like newspapers, running water, old cloths, and various spoons for mixing and stirring

PROJECT STAGES

Preparation

When you have studied the design grid (see **12-2**), and sorted out your tools and materials, take your chosen tin and check it over to make sure that its in sound condition. This done, give it a quick sanding with the finest-grade sandpaper, and wipe up the dust.

Spend time looking at our designs and drawing them to size to fit the various sides of your chosen tin. Note how we have the main design set within a circle, a brushwork repeat running around the rim of the lid, and a single brushwork motif on the lid at top center.

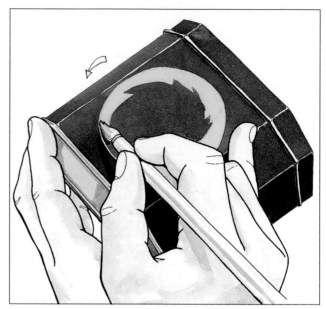

12-3   Wait until the ground paint is dry, and then block in the cream circle.

Laying On the Ground

With the tin well prepared, and the drawings pinned up so that they are within easy view, then painting can begin.

Start by decanting a small amount of the blue vinyl/latex paint. If the paint is overly thin, pour off some of the free liquid. Add a small amount of the black ink, and stir to a well-blended mix. Aim for a smooth, free-running consistency, and a color that you might describe as being a very dark, almost black-blue. Give the entire outside of the tin a couple of well-brushed coats to cover. Wipe the paint from the rolled lips—so that the underlying glow of the tin shines through—and put the tin to one side to dry.

Draw crossed diagonals to establish the center point of the side panels. Take the compass, set it to a diameter to suit your selected tin—ours is set to 1¼″— and draw a circle, one at the front and one at the back. If you are working with a tin that is a completely different shape—say a simple cylinder or maybe a multisided form, then modify the design, and draw the circles to fit.

Being satisfied with the position of the circles, take a Japanese brush, and block them in with a coat of the cream-colored vinyl/latex paint. The easiest way of blocking in is to work from inside the circle (see **12-3**). That is, paint to the drawn line, and then fill in. Lay on two or more coats to cover.

Setting Out the Design

In the context of painting a brushwork design—meaning a design that is characterized by its loose and free style—it's best if you keep the setting out to the minimum. To this end, refresh your eye by having a good long look at the design grid (see **12-2**), and then take a soft pencil and set the tin out with a series of guide marks. Don't draw in every curve and stroke, but rather simply quarter the circle, draw in the curves of the large flower at the center of the circle, maybe make a few marks to fix the position of the motif in the middle of the lid, decide how many motifs are going to run around the side of the lid, and then leave it at that.

Painting the Design

With the ground colors in place, and a series of pencil guide marks drawn out, start by mixing the deep ochre color. Squeeze a pool of PVA woodworking glue into a throwaway container, add a good dab of gouache, and blend to mix. When you are pleased with the mix, then carefully block in the large flower (see **12-2,** top left). The procedure is much the same as blocking in the circle. That is, use a small brush to carefully paint to the drawn line—so that the eight petal shapes are nicely established—and then block in the center. Once again, lay on enough coats to cover.

Wait until the ochre flower is dry, and then use a fine-point brush and the red acrylic paint to detail the edges (see **12-4**). The best procedure is to pick out the

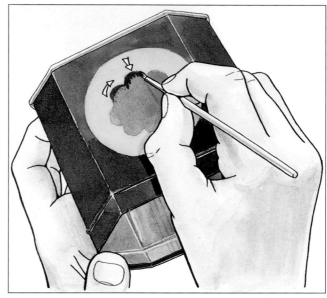

12-4   Paint the red feathered edge to the central flower.

edge shape of the flower with a red line, and then make a series of almost dry-brush strokes that run from the edge towards the center. Aim for a red edge that is about ¼″ at its widest and that fades out to paints on the inner edge of each crescent.

While the red, cream, and ochre colors are at hand, pick out the cream and ochre strokes that go to make up the lid motif, the ochre petals at each side of the center-of-circle flower, and so on (see **12-5**).

12-5   Paint the cream brush-stroke petals on the lid motif.

12-6   *Paint the dark green details on the leaves.*

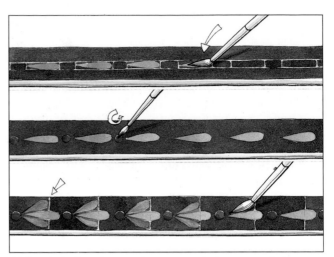

12-7   *Painting the running repeat design around the lid—(from top to bottom) paint the line of ochre dashes, dot in the red between the dashes, and finally paint the green side petals.*

To paint the leaves, block the whole leaf shape in with the light green, let it dry, and paint one half of the leaf with the darker shade of green (see **12-6**). To paint the running design around the lid, first paint the series of ochre dash strokes, paint in the red between-stroke dots, and then the two side strokes. Work with an easy action so that each stroke is created by the swift down-on-and-off action of the loaded brush (see **12-7**). Finally, use your smallest fine-point brush and the blue-black paint to pick out the little vein lines (see **12-8**).

And so you proceed, painting the delicate tendrils that curl out from the flower (see **12-9**), painting the red dot at the center of the lid motif, painting the smaller flower at the center of the large flower, dotting the red berries, and so on. Continue adding and tidying up brush strokes until you have what you consider is a fresh, crisp immediate design.

12-8   *Use a very-fine-point brush to paint in the black details.*

12-9   *Use the very-fine brush to dot in the red berries/flowers.*

Finishing

When you have achieved what you figure is a good design—one that is balanced and crisp—sign and date the bottom of the tin, and put it to one side to dry.

Finally, give the whole tin a couple of coats of varnish. Lay on one coat, let it dry, give the surface a sanding with the finest grade of sandpaper, and then lay on another coat.

AFTERTHOUGHTS

• If your found tin looks to be slightly rusty, give it a quick sanding, wipe it over with a spirit-dampened cloth, and give it a coat of metal primer.
• If you like the idea of the project, but are not so keen on the blue-black ground color, then you could go for another traditional color like deep red, yellow, dark green, or brown-black.

• If you decide to use black paint straight from the can, then make sure that you use matt black.
• If you do decide to restore, say, your great-granny's coffee pot, then first make certain that it isn't a piece of valuable early Pennsylvania ware.
• If you plan to use your ware for containing food, then make doubly certain that all your paints are non-toxic.
• A mix of white PVA wood glue and either powder pigment or gouache paint makes a really sound, semi-gloss paint.
• Perhaps more than anything else, brushwork designs are characterized by the feeling that they have been dashed off effortlessly, with the minimum of setting out. If you are a beginner, you could work towards achieving a "swift" image by having a number of pre-project tryouts. Experiment with brush strokes—try to reduce the motif to a small number of direct strokes.

—13—
Angels and Tulips Chest of Drawers

THE PARTICULARLY EXCITING thing about the Pennsylvania German folk artists is that they never really lost touch with their old-world customs and traditions. So, for example, when they were painting more or less run-of-the-mill furniture in the nineteenth century, they were still using traditional old-world dower chest symbols that harked back to early eighteenth-century German and Swiss peasant designs. Certainly by this time, many of the motifs were so stylized that they were barely recognizable, and no doubt the painters had very little understanding any longer of the symbolic significance of what it was they were painting— the forms, colors, and details—but nevertheless the thread that linked the Old World to the New remained unbroken.

13-1   Project picture—the finished chest of drawers, with angels, tulips, corner fans, and striped bevels.

96

13-2 A   Design grid—four squares to 1". (Top) Design for small drawer—to the centerline. (Bottom left) Piece of card 1½" to 1¾" for printing the fan.

13-2 B   Design grid—at a scale of four grid squares to 1". Design for the larger drawer—note the increased height of the tulip stem and the extra leaf.

We have drawn the inspiration for this project from an undated Pennsylvania chest that was probably made and decorated in the third quarter of the nineteenth century. When we look at this design, we are excited by the notion that the painter was, as it were, not only using the traditional motifs more as abstract shapes than as meaningful symbols, but more than that, was experimenting with color, and possibly stencilling. This is in no way to take anything away from the work—in fact just the opposite. When we look at this design, we see the work of a dynamic, uninhibited new-world painter who was really enjoying the juicy pleasure of playing around with abstract blocks of color and pattern.

If you look at the project picture (see **13-1**) and other illustrations, you will note that the design explores the techniques of color transposition for the motifs, and paint printing for the corner fans.

CHOOSING THE PAINTS, COLORS, MATERIALS, AND BRUSHES

This project uses a milk paint wash for the ground, acrylics for the design motifs and the printing, a tinted wax varnish for a glaze, and beeswax for the finish.

We used a 1½" household paintbrush for the ground and the varnishing, and a selection of sable watercolor brushes throughout.

MATERIALS

You will need—

• a plain pine chest of drawers to decorate
• a sheet of workout and tracing paper to fit the drawer sizes
• a pencil and ruler

- a pack of graded sandpapers
- a quantity of nonfat milk powder
- a quantity of raw umber powder paint pigment, or gouache poster paint
- acrylic paints in the colors brick red, cream, blue-black, and antique white
- a selection of large, medium, and small soft-haired, sable watercolor brushes
- a small household brush for the ground and for varnishing
- a quantity of best-quality wax varnish
- a small tube of raw umber artist's quality oil-based paint
- mineral/white spirit
- a piece of cardboard for printing the fans
- a knife and metal straightedge for cutting the cardboard
- a quantity of beeswax furniture polish
- all the usual around-the-house items like newspapers, running water, old cloths, and various spoons for mixing and stirring

PROJECT STAGES

Preparation

Start by giving your found chest of drawers a good looking over. Make repairs, remove unsuitable fixings, and generally make good and bring to order. In our case we had to repair a leg, reglue one of the drawer sides, and ease out a good number of nails that the last owner had, for some reason, banged hither and thither over the front of the drawers.

Having revived the chest of drawers to the extent that it stands fair and square and the drawers slide in and out, spend time stripping off paint and/or varnish. We were lucky in that our chest had already been stripped. This done, work through the pack of graded sandpapers, sanding the surface down to a smooth finish.

Laying On the Ground

When you have before you a plain wood chest—with the drawers removed—then comes the good fun of mixing and applying the milk paint wash. Take about one cup of milk powder and mix with cold water until you have a thin syrup. Spend time blending out all the lumps. Next add the raw umber powder paint, or the gouache, to the mix until you have a thin, brown wash. You should finish up with a thin, slightly sticky mix—

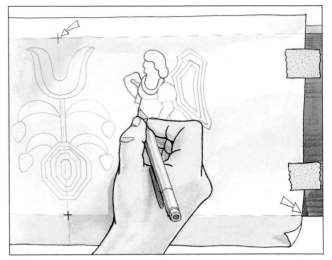

13-3   *Align the tracing with the centerline and base line, fix with tabs of masking tape, and use a hard pencil to press-transfer the traced lines onto the wood.*

a bit like cold cocoa. Try the colorwash on a piece of wood and let it dry. As needed, add more water to modify the consistency, more milk powder to adjust the opacity, or more pigment to adjust the density of the color.

Take a soft household brush, and lay on a single coat. Don't scrub around or try to work the wash into the wood, simply brush the wash on in the direction of the grain. When it is dry, sand it with the finest-grade sandpaper until it is smooth to the touch. Repeat the wash and the sanding until you have the desired color quality. Aim for an all-over medium-brown color, with the underlying texture of the grain being subtly visible—not so thick that it looks treacly, nor so thin that the wood looks starved and bleached. Finally, take a fold of fine-grade sandpaper and sand through at natural "wear" areas—on edges and corners—so as to create an aged-and-scratched much-worn effect.

Setting Out the Design

When you have, as it were, prepared your chest of drawers "canvas," stop awhile and see how we have used the designs (see 13-1). Note the way we have decorated the three long drawers with the motifs and the corner fans, and the two small top drawers with just the fans. And of course if your chest has two long drawers, more small drawers, or whatever, then consider how you will need to modify the design to fit. Study the design grids (see 13-2, A and B).

13-4   Painting the areas of cream.

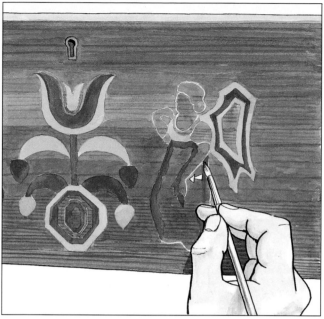

13-5   Painting the areas of red—use a fine brush to establish the edges of the drawn shape, and then block in with a larger brush.

Draw the design to size and make clear tracings. Establish the center points of the drawers by drawing crossed diagonals, and generally draw in as many guidelines as you think are necessary. Reverse your tracings so that the pencil side is looking to the wood, align them with the guideline, and fix them in place with tabs of masking tape (see **13-3**). Press-transfer the imagery through onto the wood. Last, remove the tracing and rework the lines so that they are clear and positive.

Painting the Design

With all the imagery in place, stop awhile and have a look at the project picture, design grids, and the other illustrations. Note how the painting technique is slightly unusual in that the images are made up of flat blocks of color—meaning that the colors aren't painted one on top of another, nor are the overlapping details edged in with a black line. For example, there is no attempt to suggest form lines on the front arm or around the curve of the chin.

When you have a clear picture in your mind of how the project needs to be worked, stir your paints, select suitable-sized brushes, and then to work. Start by blocking in all the areas of cream (see **13-4**)—all the dress shapes and tulip petals on one drawer, all the wings on another, and so on. The procedure is pretty straightforward; all you do is outline with a fine-point brush, and then block in with a larger brush.

With the cream areas nicely blocked in, follow through and block in the red (see **13-5**), and then the blue-black (see **13-6**), and finally the white. As needed, lay on extra coats to cover, and use the fine-point brush to tidy up the edges.

13-6   Block in the areas of black.

13-7   When you are striping the bevelled/rounded edges of the drawers, use the little finger of your brush hand as a brace. If you make a mistake, wipe the paint off with a damp cloth and start over.

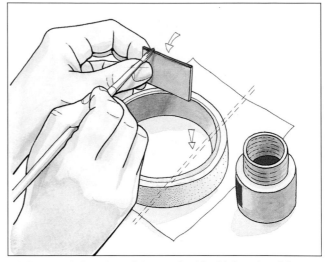

13-8   Load the edge of the card with thick paint. Note how we use the roll of tape as a brush rest between loadings.

Take a medium-size flat brush, and run a cream stripe around the bevelled edges of all the drawers. Using your small finger to steady the brush, and having first mixed the paint to a good flowing consistency, very carefully edge all the drawers (see **13-7**).

Being ready to print the corner fans, first of all note that the size of the fan will, of course, relate to the size of your chosen drawers. Ours have a radius of about 1¾″ (see **13-2 A,** bottom left). Assuming you are going for a 1¾″ radius, get yourself a little piece of packaging card, and use a metal straightedge and a craft knife to cut the card to size.

Special Tip The card gets floppy after a couple of fans have been printed, so cut half a dozen pieces.

The printing procedure is wonderfully simple: all you do is brush the edge of the card with the red paint (see **13-8**)—it's best if the paint is slightly thicker than usual—align the card so that one edge is pivoted on the corner of the drawer, and then press it down and lift it off (see **13-9**). If all is well, the card will have made a characteristic, slightly splodgy printed mark. I started by printing the edges of the fan—to make a right angle—and then filled in with subsequent prints to create the fan shape. The secret is to have the paint slightly thicker than usual, to make the mark with a positive on-and-off action, and to reload the card for each print.

Finishing

Once you have achieved all of the imagery that goes to make up the design—the angels, tulips, edge striping, and the printed fans—wash the brushes and clear the decks ready for action.

Decant what you estimate is enough wax varnish for the job, add a worm of umber oil-based paint and a very small dash of mineral/white spirit, and gently stir to make a gold-tinted varnish glaze. This done, take a wide, soft brush, and lay on a couple of coats that run in the direction of the grain. Be very careful that the

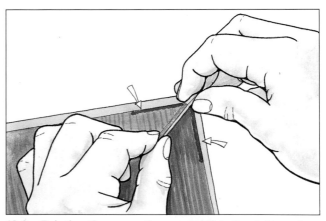

13-9   Printing the corner fans—establish the right angle, then repeatedly split the angle until you have about twelve printings for each fan.

glaze doesn't dribble. Finally, when the varnish is good and dry, give the whole chest of drawers a rub-over with a wax polish and burnish to a dull-sheen finish.

AFTERTHOUGHTS

• When you are searching for a suitable chest of drawers to decorate, it's best to go for a simple unadorned piece of old pine. Avoid anything that has been veneered, carved, oiled, or is made of an exotic hardwood such as mahogany.

• The success of this project hinges on the blocks of color that go to make up the design being flat and clean-cut, with an absence of texture and brush strokes. Don't be tempted to use gloss paint.

• If possible, remove the handles before painting—we couldn't because they were glued in place.

— 14 —
Tulips and Vase Wash Trough

THE EARLY PENNSYLVANIA German kitchen cum living room was at the center of all the important household activities. With its stove, large table, and collection of stools and chairs, it was where just about everything happened, from cooking, eating, and washing, to sewing, gun cleaning, and simply sitting around the stove or fire after a long day's work.

The wonderful thing was that within what was without a doubt a pretty modest, make-do-and-mend situation, the members of the family either spent time themselves painting and decorating many of the objects of daily use, or at least payed a travelling painter to do it for them. Every hausfrau required that even the most humble brush and box be decorated with characteristic flowers and motifs.

Our wash trough draws its inspiration from a dough trough dated about 1820 to 1830—this is a slant sided box where dough was left to prove and rise. We spotted our trough at a local farm auction, full of old tools and various rusty items.

14-1 Project picture—the finished trough.

Although our box is a wash trough (see **14-1**), rather than a dough trough, no matter, it's a beautiful country piece. Better still, we picked it up for the give-away price of the rusty tools.

You might well not be able to come up with a trough, but then again, you could just as well decorate a found chest, a tool box, or whatever. If the hausfrau was happy to have her wash bucket and broom painted, then there's no reason why you can't decorate some equally workaday item.

Albeit we have more or less left the box in its original state—we feel that the rusty nails and the old dabs of filler bear honest witness to its past—we have ever so slightly exaggerated the feeling of age by sanding through the paint at "wear" points.

CHOOSING THE PAINTS, COLORS, MATERIALS, AND BRUSHES

Having said that this project uses the very simplest of paint and materials—powder pigment milk paint for the ground, flat ceiling white for the panel, and acrylics for the painted imagery—it does require extra time and effort at the preparation and ground-painting stages.

We used a full range of brushes, everything from ordinary household brushes for the ground to sables and Japanese calligraphy brushes for the imagery.

MATERIALS

You will need—

• a suitable found box or container to decorate—ours measures about 27″ long, 12″ high, and 15″ wide
• a sheet each of workout and tracing paper to fit the front of the box
• a pencil and ruler
• a pack of graded sandpapers
• a quantity of instant nonfat milk powder
• a quantity of powder water paint pigment, as used by schools—in the color yellow-green—sometimes called yellow-Brunswick green
• white flat vinyl/latex paint, as used on ceilings
• acrylic paints in the colors red, chrome-yellow, green, raw umber, and black
• a 1″ domestic brush for laying on the ground
• a selection of sable and Japanese brushes for the details
• a collection of throwaway cans and jars

14-2 Design grid—at a scale of approximately three grid squares to 1″. Since the design is symmetrical, you can, if you wish, only draw and trace the design up to the centerline.

• all the usual around-the-house items like newspapers, running water, old cloths, and various old spoons for mixing and stirring

PROJECT STAGES

Preparation
Take your found box, and use a stiff brush to remove loose paint. This done, give the box a good looking over just to make sure that it's in sound structural condition. After all, there's not much point in spending time, if the box is so riddled with worm and rot that it's going to blow away in the first breeze. If you look closely at our illustrations, you will see that we replaced the floor runners.

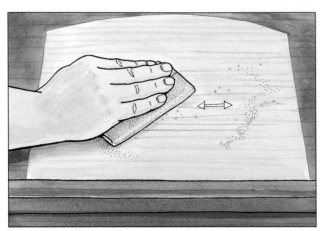

14-3   Cut through the white ground by sanding with a fold of fine-grade sandpaper—work in the direction of the grain.

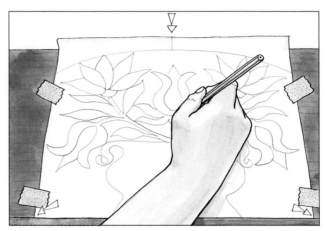

14-4   Align the tracing with the centerline and base line, fix it secure with masking tape, and use a hard pencil to press-transfer the design onto the white ground.

Special Tip A good part of the secret of painting found items like chests and boxes is to know just how far to take the preparation. Our best advice is to do as little as possible. Okay, *something* does need to be done if the lid or whatever is so rotten that it's about to crumble away, or if the piece is in any way dangerous, but otherwise leave well enough alone.

When you have done no more than remove splinters, ease out nails, and maybe filled splits, then use the fine-grade sandpaper to sand the wood to a smooth finish. Work in the direction of the grain, all the while doing your best to give emphasis to areas that are worn.

If a repair has to be done, then you have to make a choice as to whether you are going to try to disguise the mend, or draw attention to it by using what might be called "naive" or "eccentric" fixing. For example, we've seen old boxes that have been fixed with straps of brass. And then again, we've seen a box that was patched with a large enamelled advertising sign.

With all the preparations complete, clean up the mess, and wipe the box over with a damp cloth.

Laying On the Ground

Take ½ cup of nonfat milk powder, add water, and blend until you have a thick syrup. As needed, add more powder or water to mix. Ideally it needs to have the consistency of runny honey. When you have stirred and blended the mix, add the yellow-green powder paint little by little, until you have a nice, smooth

paint. Have a tryout, and then add more color, more milk, or more water, as the case may be.

When you have what you consider is a paint mix of the right color, density, and consistency, then take your chosen item and lay on a single thin coat. Note how we have limited our painting to the outside and edges, and paint your item accordingly. Wait for the paint to dry, and then rub the whole surface down to a smooth finish. Once again, cut through the paint and areas of wear—meaning the edges and corners. This done, repeat the procedure three or four times, until you have a good, dense, flat finish.

14-5   Use a large brush to block in the remaining area of black.

14-6   *Use a medium-fine brush to paint the green leaves and stalks.*

14-7   *Paint the yellow petals.*

Finally, mix a small dab of acrylic raw umber with water—until you have a thin muddy wash—and wipe the painted surface to achieve a surface that looks to be slightly aged. Concentrate your efforts on areas that ought, in the normal course of events, to be soiled—around the handles, above and below moulding and rims, and so on.

Setting Out the Design

Start by studying the design grid (see **14-2**). Having drawn the panel design to full size and made a clear tracing, spend time with a pencil and ruler setting out a centerline and base line. Fix the center by drawing crossed diagonals, and draw the base line about 1″ up from the bottom of the item.

Reverse the tracing so that the pencil side is looking to the item, align it with the guidelines, and fix it in place with tabs of masking tape. When you are sure that the placing is correct, use a pencil and ruler to press-transfer the shape of the panel to the wood. Don't bother at this stage with the motif.

With the shape of the panel in place, block it in with the flat white paint. Lay on one or more coats for a smooth, dense cover. It's important that the edges of the panel are as crisp and as clear as possible; so spend time getting it right.

Wait until the white is completely dry, then take a sheet of fine-grade sandpaper, and sand the whole face of the item (see **14-3**). Blur the edges of the white panel, and cut through the white so that you can see the underlying texture of the wood and the green ground.

Finally, realign the tracing paper, and press-transfer the vase and flower imagery onto the white panel (see **14-4**).

Painting the Design

With the design in place, take brushes and the acrylic colors—red, chrome-yellow, green, and black, and set to work blocking in the design. The order of work is to block in the black vase (see **14-5**), the green stems (see **14-6**), and the chrome-yellow petals (see **14-7**), and last paint in the red petals and the decorative red dots on the yellow petals (see **14-8**). As needed, lay on second coats to cover.

14-8   *Finish by dotting in the red paint on the yellow petals.*

Finishing

As for finishing, what could be easier—a wipe-over with the raw umber wash, another swift all-over sanding to slightly blur and break up the colors, and the project is finished.

AFTERTHOUGHTS

• Since some old pieces are decorated with toxic lead paints, be sure to wear a dust mask, and vacuum up the sanding dust. If the box is in a real mess with lots of thick and peeling lead paint, then consider having it professionally stripped.

• As with all the other projects, if you do manage to find a really old piece, then have a specialist evaluate it before you start the sanding and painting.

• If you are worried about your milk paint going mouldy, you can add a small amount of antifungal wall paper glue to the mix.

—15—
Freehand Brush-Stroke Painted Tinware

W HEN WE THINK of Pennsylvania tinware, we imagine peddlers setting out their fancy painted and decorated wagons loaded down with stock—coffee pots, pitchers, mugs, measuring cups, money boxes, and much more. We can almost hear the tinware clinking as the wagons bump and bounce their way westwards across the Great Plains. And then again, we see all the womenfolk gathering around—lots of gossip and excited chatter—as the peddler arrives at a village and starts trading.

Our imaginings may be a bit "technicolored," and no doubt various historians are going to say that Pennsylvania tin was only traded up to Canada, or only by canal, or whatever, and in very general terms that's pretty much the way it was. Pennsylvania tinware was so inexpensive, and popular, and widely marketed, that just about every nineteenth-century American household could lay claim to having at least one piece.

15-1   Project picture—the finished chest.

Once we decided to do this project, we had in mind to decorate something really big. Perhaps a deed/document box, or maybe a hat or cookie box. In the end, we were lucky enough to find what we were told was "a live-in maid trunk," made around 1900. As to when and where it was actually made, who knows? To us it looks very European—maybe English? All we do know for sure is that it is made of tin, it was originally decorated and grained to imitate leather, and it is almost certainly at least a hundred years old. All in all, it was just perfect!

Good advice, when you are searching out items to decorate, is to visit antique fairs, country auctions, flea markets, and church bazaars, and to keep your eyes open. Just about every cellar, attic, rubbish dump, old house, and garden shed is a potential treasury!

It's unlikely that you will be able to obtain an identical item, so it's best to use our project as a guide, and modify the details accordingly.

CHOOSING THE PAINTS, COLORS, MATERIALS, AND BRUSHES

Traditionally, Pennsylvania tin painters favored bold, bright, punchy colors—black, brownish black, blue, and cream—for the ground, and just about the whole range for the details. This project uses a varnish glaze to enhance the original, rather tired brown ground, and acrylics in the colors red, chrome-yellow, cream, and light, medium, and dark green for the imagery (see **15-1**).

We used a small household brush for the ground, a Japanese calligraphy brush for the large areas of color, and a selection of soft-haired, sable watercolor brushes for the details.

MATERIALS

You will need—

• a large item of tinware to decorate—a trunk, chest, or deed/document box
• a sheet of workout paper as large as the surface that you intend to decorate
• a sheet of fine-grade sandpaper
• flat acrylic paints in the colors chrome-yellow, red, cream, and three shades of leaf-green—light, medium, and dark
• three soft-haired, sable watercolor brushes in the

sizes very large, medium, and small fine-point
• a medium Japanese calligraphy brush
• a can of clear yacht/spar varnish
• a quantity of mineral/white spirit
• a small tube of umber artist's quality oil-based paint
• a tin of beeswax furniture polish
• a soft cotton cloth for polishing
• a collection of throwaway cans and jars
• all the usual around-the-house items like newspapers, running water, a pencil and ruler, old cloths, and various old spoons for mixing and stirring

PROJECT STAGES

Preparation
Starting out on the premise that you have found yourself a good-size item of old painted tin—a trunk, a cookie box, or some such, in a color like black, off-white, or brown—commence by checking it over, just to make sure that it isn't valuable in its own right. For example, if there are signs of old patterns under the topcoat, then get it checked out by a specialist.

Wipe the whole tin over with a spirit-dampened cloth, and then give it a wash in warm, soapy water. This should remove all of the grease and grime. If however, your item has at some time been splashed with flecks of flat white distemper or something similar—ours was—take a small, flat wooden stick and very carefully rub and remove the drops of paint. Try not to damage the underlying ground paint. This done, give the whole surface a very quick and light sanding with a piece of fine-grade sandpaper. Don't try to remove the finish, simply do no more than lightly abrade the surface.

Laying On the Ground
Decant enough varnish for a couple of all-over coats, add a small squeeze of umber oil paint, and a dash of mineral/white spirit, and stir together until you have a golden glaze. Set your piece up at a comfortable height, and generally spend time clearing the working area. If you are working outside, then check that it isn't going to rain or blow up a dust storm, and if you are working inside, ensure that there is plenty of ventilation.

Give your item a single coat of glaze, wipe off dribbles and runs, and leave it to dry. When it is entirely dry, give it a light sanding with the fine-grade sandpaper, followed by a wipe-down and another coat. You

15-2 *Design grid—a general guide. The brush-stroke technique is best achieved without tracing since tracing, in this instance, tends to inhibit and spoil the work. (Top left) Corner motif. (Right) Half the main design—the other half is reversed.*

will find that whatever the condition of the surface, this treatment will enhance the finish. If it is a "tired" black, or a dirty cream, or just about any color, the glaze will leave the surface looking bright and invigorated.

sketch in a small number of pencil guidelines. For example, you could make a few dots to indicate the size of the two motifs, and perhaps fix the position of the corner details. Don't go wild with the guidelines; try to keep them to a minimum.

Setting Out the Design

When you have prepared your tinware item, and given it a couple of coats of varnish glaze, then stop awhile and refresh your eye by looking at our project picture (see **15-1**) and design grid (see **15-2**). Notice the way that we have, as it were, filled the space—the front of the tin chest—by having the two primary motifs in the middle, and the small details at the corners.

Study our design grid, draw the designs to fit the size of your chosen piece, and set them alongside your working area. Fix the position of the center point—meaning on your chest/box—by drawing crossed diagonals. This done, take a soft pencil, and lightly

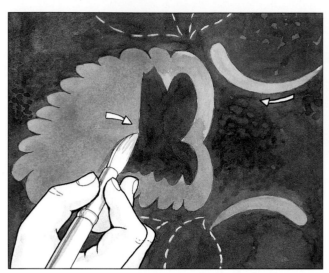

15-3   Use the large sable brush to paint in the flowers and the two long curved linking shapes.

15-4   (Top) Use the large sable brush to paint the leaves—some are half light green and half medium green, while others are all medium green. At this stage paint blocks of medium green over the light green areas. Use the fine-point brush to paint the cream outline. (Bottom) Use the medium Japanese brush to paint the dark green leaf veins and shadows.

Painting the Design

Having first spent as much time as possible practising on a sheet of paper, take a good-size sable brush and the yellow acrylic, and paint in the two large flower-like motifs. **Don't** line in the edge and then block in—as in other projects—but rather, let the loaded brush create the edge profile. Working in this way, by the time you have made a series of brush strokes down one side of the motif, followed by a series of strokes down the other, all you will then need to do is fill in the center (see **15-3**). While the yellow paint is at hand, make the two, long curved shapes that link the large areas of yellow.

The secret with freehand brush-stroke painting is to let the loaded brush more or less make its own mark. If you look at the photograph, you can actually see how the brush strokes fill out the shape. With the yellow forms painted in, take a slightly smaller brush and the light green color, and paint in the twelve, large leaf shapes (see **15-4**, top). Once again load your brush, sit awhile and study the design, and then complete each leaf with two or three heavy-pressure strokes. Our advice, if you are at all worried, is to be brave! And of course, it doesn't matter whether you make a mess-up the first time around, all you do is wipe the mistakes away with a damp cloth—before the paint dries—and start over.

With the twelve fat leaves in place, take a smaller brush—we used the Japanese brush—and, still working with the same light green color, paint in the twelve slender leaves that occur in four groups of three. Try to complete each leaf with a single, swift stroke (see **15-5**).

Once the large leaves are dry, take a medium-size brush and the medium-green color, and overpaint some leaves as shown. For example, some leaves are given an all-over coat of medium green, while others are over-painted on one side and then given a couple of swift dashes on the other side (see **15-4**, bottom). If you look at the photograph, you will see that the technique creates the impression that the leaves have three-dimensional form and depth. As soon as the medium green is dry, take a smaller brush and the dark green, and paint in the spines and shadows as shown. Once again, don't belabor the painting by making lots of hesitant fussy strokes; simply load the brush and make the brave stroke.

Once you have, as it were, mapped out the design by painting in the primary forms, take a small Japanese brush and the cream paint, and set to work painting in the petal shapes on the center flowers and the various highlights around the edges (see **15-6**). This stage is particularly exciting in that you will, at long last, be able to see the design beginning to take shape. And

15-5 *The slender leaves are best painted with a soft-haired Japanese calligraphy brush.*

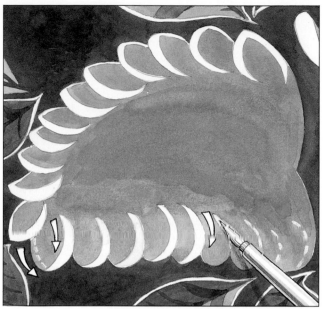

15-6 *Use the small Japanese brush and the cream paint to work the small petal shapes at the middle of the flower.*

once again, don't fidget around with jerky, hesitant strokes, simply analyze the shape, load the brush, and make the mark. When you come to painting the two fern frond shapes, first paint in the spine line with a couple of strokes, and then work down each side of the spine flicking in the small dashes (see **15-7**).

While the cream paint is at hand, change over to a slightly larger brush, and paint in the secondary strokes of cream. If at any time the paint is too thick, or the brush becomes clogged, simply wash the brush in water, add a few drops of water to the paint, and begin again.

Continue layering the brush strokes of color, one on top of another until the design is complete: red and cream brush strokes on the yellow flowers, dots of red around the cream center point, cream dots around the red dot at the center of the areas of yellow, and so on. Be mindful throughout that your aim should be to more or less let the shape of the brush create its own characteristic mark. That said, you can, of course, vary the width of the brush stroke by applying more, or less, pressure. For example, a light, swift stroke produces a thin, pointed-at-both-ends line, while a slower, heavier stroke will result in a wider, fatter, round-at-one-end mark. If at any point along the way, you have trouble, then stop awhile, clean your brush, make sure that the paint is smooth and flowing, and loosen up your wrist by having a tryout on a piece of paper.

15-7 *Use the fine brush to paint the fern-like details.*

Finally, paint in the corner motifs and the little red jewel-like details (see **15-8**). Generally go over the painting tidying up edges and details.

Finishing

Once you have completed the painting to your satisfaction—this might take anywhere from a couple of hours to a couple of days depending on your skill with a brush—sign and date the chest. When the paint is completely dry, give the whole works a last coat of clear varnish and let it re-dry.

Finally, give the entire surface a swift rubdown with wax furniture polish, and burnish to a high-shine finish.

AFTERTHOUGHTS

• If you look closely at our illustrations, you will see that our tin trunk was originally painted brown, and then combed with a wavy pattern around the rim. If you like this notion, look to the vinegar painting project, number four.

• If you are planning to decorate new tin, then it would be a good idea to start by laying down an interesting ground color and texture. Loot at the other projects for inspiration.

15-8   Use the medium-size Japanese brush to paint the red details. Notice how the little spots diminish in size as they follow the curve of the flower.

• If you like the idea of freehand brush-stroke painting, then bear in mind the old adage—''practice makes perfect.'' Our best advice is to get yourself a whole heap of empty food cans, paint them black, and then use them as tryout pieces. You could, perhaps, present the finished cans to a charity bazaar, and along the way master the painting techniques.

—16—
Strawberries and Vines
Heart-Shaped Boxes

T HIS BEAUTIFUL PROJECT was inspired by a Pennsylvania candle box made and painted in about 1800. The original design features three stylized motifs—strawberries, grapes, and red currants.

When we came to use the design, we decided to stay with the same strikingly lovely colors—brilliant yellow for the ground, red for the fruit, and green-grey for the foliage—and the same overall forms. With the original box—now in the Metropolitan Museum of Art, New York—the strawberries are on the lid, the grapes on one long side, and currants on the ends.

If you have a close-up look at our nest of four steam-bent boxes (see **16-1**), you will see that we have lifted the three primary motifs intact and simply reworked the size and grouping so that they fit the heart shape. We didn't need to mess with the forms; all we did was trace the motifs off direct—from our small research photograph—and then generally played around with the size and the arrangement until we were happy with the balance.

16-1 Project picture—the finished boxes.

113

When we came to work out the placing of the motifs within the heart shapes, we simple drew around the boxes—so that we had four heart shapes—enlarged and reduced the strawberries so that we had four slightly different sizes, and then took it from there.

The exciting thing is—and this is really quite something when you consider that the original box was painted nearly two hundred years ago—that the forms, the colors, and the layout are as fresh, as brilliant, and as dynamic as the day they were first painted.

Study the design grids (see **16-2 A** and **B**), and see how, at a grid scale of four squares to 1″, the designs relate to small hand-size boxes. Note the centerlines, the guidelines, and the design layout of the strip that runs around the lid.

CHOOSING THE PAINTS, COLORS, MATERIALS, AND BRUSHES

This project uses the very simplest of paint and materials: flat yellow acrylic for the ground, flat red and green-grey acrylics for the decoration, a clear high-shine varnish for the finish, and a swift rub-over with wax polish to reduce the squeaky friction of the varnish.

We use a selection of soft-haired, sable watercolor brushes throughout.

Special Tip If you want a softer finish, you could leave out the varnish and simply wax polish the dry, painted surface.

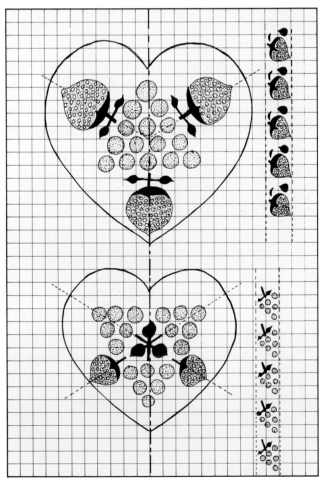

16-2 A   Design grid—at a scale of four grid squares to 1″. Two designs for lids and edges.

16-2 B   Design grid—at a scale of four grid squares to 1″. Two designs for lids and edges.

MATERIALS

You will need—

- a nest or set of boxes to decorate
- a sheet each of workout and tracing paper
- a sheet of fine-grade sandpaper
- flat acrylic paints in the colors chrome-yellow, red, and green-grey
- three soft-haired, sable watercolor brushes in the sizes large, medium, and small fine-point
- a can of clear yacht/spar varnish
- a quantity of mineral/white spirit
- a tin of beeswax furniture polish
- a soft cotton cloth for polishing
- a collection of throwaway cans and jars
- all the usual around-the-house items like newspapers, running water, a pencil and ruler, old cloths, and various old spoons for mixing and stirring

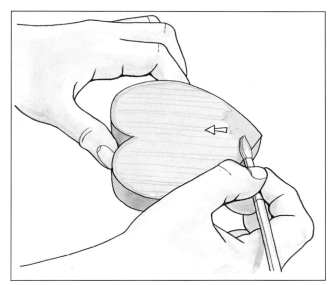

16-3   Use a large sable brush to lay on the yellow ground—start with the base and sides, and finish with the top.

PROJECT STAGES

Preparation

Take your boxes—ours are steam-bent and new—and check them over, just to make sure that they are in good sound condition. If the wood looks to be absorbent, lay on a thin coat of varnish to seal the grain. Sand the boxes to remove grain hairs and nibs, and generally bring the surface of the wood to good order.

Special Tip With thin steam-bent boxes, you do have to be very careful not to sand through the wood thickness.

If you have chosen to use found boxes—say a set of cigar boxes, something like a trinket box, or whatever—then spend time making certain that the surface is sound. So, for example, you might strip off paper labels, wipe wax polish off with mineral/white spirit, or fill cracks, and so forth. If the surface is in any way sticky, first wipe it over with a mineral-spirit-dampened cloth, then lay on a coat of varnish, let it dry, and have a tryout with the acrylics. If the paint stays put, then fine, but if the surface remains sticky, a stain comes through the paint, or the acrylics pucker, then cut your losses and look for another box.

Laying On the Ground

When you have achieved one or more boxes, all nicely rubbed down, cleaned, and sealed, then wipe them over with a damp cloth to remove dust, and move to the area set aside for painting.

Spend time working out just how you are going to support the boxes once they have been painted. For example, you might place them rim-side-down on wooden boards, lift them up from the worksurface by setting them on small throwaway containers, or set each box/lid up with three stainless-steel pin legs—there are many options. It's important that you know what you are going to do with the boxes once they have been painted.

Start by mixing enough acrylic paint to cover. Using the large brush, lay on a single, thin, well-brushed coat (see **16-3**)—around the sides, around the edges, and on the top and the base. When the first coat is dry, take the boxes away from the painting area and give them another quick sanding to remove recalcitrant whiskers of grain.

Last, having given the surface a wipe-over with a damp cloth, lay on another coat of yellow, and then put the boxes to one side to dry.

Special Tip If the boxes are made of very thin wood, it's a good idea to stabilize the structure by painting inside the boxes.

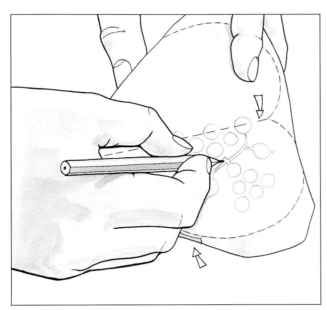

16-4   *Align the tracing with the centerline and the heart shape; hinge it in place with tabs of masking tape. Carefully pencil-press-transfer the design onto the painted ground.*

Setting Out the Design

Having finalized the design and drawn it to size, use a soft pencil to make clear tracings.

Special Tip Tracing paper comes in several thicknesses or grades. Certainly you can use the thinnest, but we prefer using the best-quality grade. The heavy-duty paper is comfortable to handle, while the thinnest tends to wrinkle, tear, and generally be a nuisance. We figure that the best-quality paper goes farthest!

Take a soft pencil, and set each box out with a centerline and as many guidelines as you think helpful. So, for example, if you look at our design grids, you will see that some designs are set out with 120-degree angles radiating from a center point, while one design needs no more than a centerline.

With the guidelines in place, reverse the symmetrical tracings so that the drawn lines are looking to the wood, align them with the guidelines, and fix them in place with tabs of masking tape. Note that, if you decide to go for an asymmetrical design, then you will have to overdraw the back of the tracing and afterwards press-transfer with the back of the tracing looking towards the wood.

Use hard pencil or ballpoint pen to press-transfer the traced imagery onto the working face of the wood (see **16-4**).

Painting the Design

With the design in place, and having mixed your paints to a good smooth consistency and selected your brushes—we used a fine-point—then the fun can begin. Start by blocking in the red (see **16-5**)—for the red strawberries, red grapes, and red currants. Keep the lines clean, and, as needed, lay on a second coat to cover. Work from box to box, filling in the areas of red.

When the red is dry, take the fine brush and the green-grey paint, and very carefully line in the small details that go to make the vines, sepals, and leaves (see **16-6**). Work with a swift clean stroke, all the while trying to achieve lines that are immediate and unworried. The sequence for painting a shape like a leaf is to make a single stroke for the stalk, make a brush stroke at each side to define the shape of the leaf, and then complete the shape by blocking in.

Special Tip If you are at all unsure how to paint a form, or perhaps have a shaky hand, then it might be just as well, prior to the project, to have a tryout on some scrap wood. Make repeated strokes until you achieve a smooth, loose-wristed action.

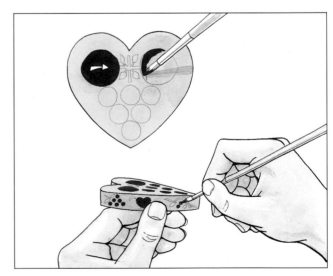

16-5   *(Top) When you are blocking in the red strawberries, paint straight over the area that will eventually be painted green. (Bottom) Use a fine-point brush to paint the edge-of-lid designs.*

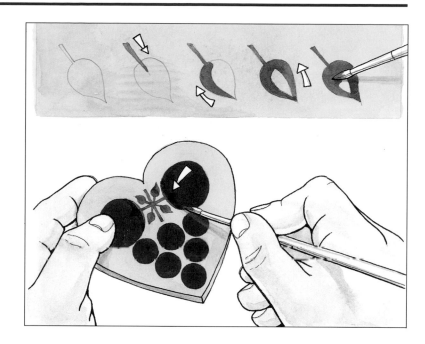

16-6 (Top, left to right) The arrow indicating the position of the brush; the order for painting a leaf is paint the stalk, paint first one side of the leaf and then the other, finish by blocking in. (Bottom) Use a small brush and the green color to overpaint the red areas at the top of the strawberry to create the calyx leaf-cap.

Finally, when both the red and the green-grey colors are dry, take your smallest brush and the yellow paint, and dot in the decorative pattern on the strawberries (see **16-7**).

Finishing
Being sure that the acrylic paints are thoroughly dry, take the large brush and the varnish, and, starting with the sides, give all the painted surfaces a couple of thin, flowing coats (see **16-8**). Lay on one coat, let it dry, give it a quick sanding with the fine-grade sandpaper, and lay on another coat.

Last, when the varnish is good and dry, give all the surfaces a wipe-over with wax polish, and burnish to a soft-shine finish.

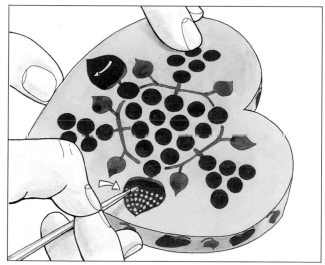

16-7 Use a fine-point brush to paint the strawberry pips—arrange the lines of pips so that they describe the curved shape of the fruit.

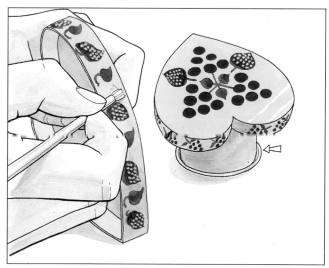

16-8 When you are varnishing, start with the sides and finish with the lid/base—make sure that you brush away all runs and dribbles.

AFTERTHOUGHTS

• If you like the project, but would prefer to use oil-based paints, then be prepared for the long wait between coats.

• If, by chance, you have a collection of gloss acrylics, then be aware that they are very difficult to use. Gloss paints of this character can't easily be set down one on top of another—they slide about and are difficult to cover.

• Preparing the painting area is all-important. If you are organized, with supports for the objects once they have been painted, and old cloths for wiping your brushes, and so forth, then the project will run smoothly. But then again, if the work surface is covered in dust and clutter, and you are being worried by the phone, the dog, or something else, then be ready for disaster.

• If you are working with children, or your children want to watch, don't shoo them away, but rather sit them down, get them settled and equipped, and then show them how it's done.

—17—
Tortoiseshelling

THE PENNSYLVANIA PAINTERS greatly enjoyed using novel combinations of varnish and oil paint to create wild and exciting effects. Tortoiseshelling, sometimes called turtle work, is one such technique (see **17-1**).

Although at first sight tortoiseshelling looks to be hugely involved and unpredictable, it is in fact a relatively straightforward, almost foolproof, technique. The area to be decorated is given a coat of flat orange-yellow paint and allowed to dry. The dry surface is given a coat of dark varnish, oil paints; then artist's black and umber tube colors are streaked over the freshly varnished ground; and finally the whole works is stroked this way and that with a dry brush. The finished surface is a wonderfully rich and exotic imitation of tortoiseshell.

17-1   Project picture—a cupboard with tortoiseshelled panels.

17-2   Lay on the flat, bright orange-yellow ground color.

MATERIALS

You will need—

• a surface to decorate—we have chosen to decorate door panels, but you could just as well go for a chest, a tabletop, or whatever
• a pack of graded sandpapers
• a quantity of flat vinyl/latex paint in an orange-yellow color
• a couple of soft-haired, sable watercolor brushes—a broad- and a fine-point
• a couple of ½″ wide household brushes
• a can of clear, medium oak varnish
• a quantity of mineral/white spirit
• two tubes of artist's quality oil paint, in the colors umber and black
• a collection of throwaway cans and jars
• all the usual around-the-house items like newspapers, running water, old cloths, and various spoons for mixing

When we first had a go at tortoiseshelling—described in some old books as "faux natural turtle-shelling"—we must admit that it was a dismal mess. The finish was almost completely black, and slightly sticky—like a child's well-licked stick of liquorice! The good news, is—you will be glad to hear—we eventually got the technique figured out. But just so that you don't make our mistakes, the secret lies in the color of the orange-yellow ground coat—it needs to be very bright—and in not using too much oil paint. Certainly at first sight having your favorite cabinet or other furniture item painted an orange-yellow custard color is a bit daunting, but not to panic, because it's very soon transformed into a rich gold-brown finish.

If you look at our working stages, and then at the end result, you will see that the finish is truly beautiful. That said, it is our belief that tortoiseshelling is so rich that it is best limited to relatively small areas.

CHOOSING THE PAINTS, COLORS, MATERIALS, AND BRUSHES

Although tortoiseshelling can be worked with a base other than orange-yellow, we think that, in the first instance, it's advisable to stay with the natural colors. You could, perhaps, consider variations once you have achieved a certain amount of expertise. By "flat" yellow we mean a paint of the vinyl/latex type.

PROJECT STAGES

Preparation

Once you have a clear understanding of the working stages—what needs to be done, and when—then sand your surface to a smooth finish. Don't worry too much about old paint, but do make sure that the surface is free from oil, grease, putty, and the like. Remove loose material, set nailheads below the surface, and fill cracks. Being mindful that the technique is that much easier if the surface is in the horizontal plane, you could unscrew doors and set them up on trestles.

Laying On the Ground

Having made sure that everything is ready to go, take the household brush and the flat yellow paint, and give the surface to be decorated a swift all-over coat (see **17-2**). Don't worry too much about the direction of the brush strokes, just make sure that you achieve a smooth surface. As needed, lay on a second coat to cover.

When the paint is completely dry, take the second household brush and the medium oak varnish, and give the yellow a single swift coat. Once again, don't worry too much, in the first instance, about the direction of the brush strokes or the quality of the spread; just make sure that the yellow is covered.

17-3   Use the medium brush to paint the 1½" to 2" "worms" of umber oil-based paint over the varnished and varnish-smudged, flat orange-yellow ground.

Painting the Design

As soon as possible after the surface has been varnished, brush it in a diagonal direction—from corner to corner—so that it looks to have a grain. This done, take the brush and the varnish, and make a series of daubs along the diagonal run of the varnish grain. Figure on a fairly random spread, with the daubs being about 2" to 3" apart.

Take the burnt umber and a small brush, and paint a series of wriggly worms that appear to be moving in the same direction as the grain (see **17-3**). Once again, don't be too fussy, just get the paint down as swiftly as possible. Aim to have the irregular lines of worms about 1" apart. Next, take the black oil-based color, and paint little dabs and daubs in areas that looks to be empty (see **17-4**)—that is to say, between the daubs of varnish and the painted worms. If all is correct, the daubs, worms, and splodges should seem to be "moving" in the same diagonal direction.

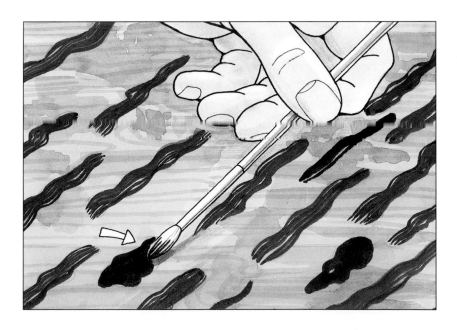

17-4   Dab little pools of black oil-based color in the spaces—aim for a fairly random spread.

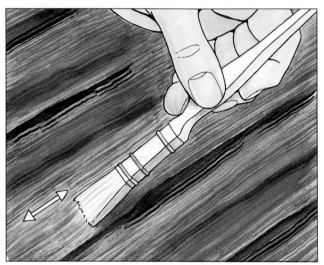

17-5 *Use the ½"-wide dry brush to blend and soften the colors—work one way and then the other.*

Finishing

And now for the exciting make-or-break bit! Take one of the ½" household brushes—make sure that it is clean and dry—and gently stroke the surface so as to brush in the opposite direction to the various blobs and squiggles. So, for example, if your squiggles run from bottom left through to top right, then stroke the dry brush from bottom right to top left. This done, repeat the brushing, only this time go in the same direction as the blobs and squiggles (see **17-5**).

And so you continue, rerunning the procedure, first one way and then the other—three or four times—until you have what you consider is a good overall color and texture. Last, finish up by brushing in the direction of the original blobs and worms.

Special Tip If you want to go for a super-subtle finish, then continue the dry-brushing until all the colors more or less blend.

AFTERTHOUGHTS

• If you are a beginner—you might have a preproject tryout on a panel of scrap wood.
• If you plan to do a very large surface, then either break the area up into manageable sections and emphasize the breaks by running the "grain" in opposite directions, or get a couple of friends to help.
• Don't overdo the size of the worms of oil paint—meaning the amount of paint. If you use too much oil paint, the drying time will be greatly extended.

—18—
Unicorn Dower Chest

O F ALL THE projects in this book, I think that the unicorn chest is, without a doubt, one of our personal favorites. To our thinking, the bold colors, the striking imagery, and the wonderfully confident brushwork just about sum up the best of the best of the Pennsylvania tradition.

The old-time painter, busy working on a chest like this, didn't pull any punches—everything the artist had went into the composition. The design is amazingly powerful (see **18-1**).

This project draws its inspiration from a group of dower chests that were made and decorated in Berks County, Pennsylvania, between about 1790 and 1803. All the chests have more or less the same layout, that is, three arch-top panels, heraldic unicorns on the central panel, horsemen on the side panels, and stylized tulip vines growing from vases, with all three panels bordered by zigzag triangles and dots and dashes. Of course, from chest to chest the details vary; but we're prepared to wager that all three chests were either painted by the same hand, or at the very least, painted by a family "team."

18-1   Project picture—the finished chest.

If you would like to see the originals, one chest is in the Philadelphia Museum, two more are in the Henry Francis du Pont Winterthur Museum, and no doubt there are other examples to be found in the major city museums.

Our chest measures 23″ from front to back, 41″ long, and 20″ high. Note the symmetrical layout of the total design, of the central panel, and of a good many individual motifs.

CHOOSING THE PAINTS, COLORS, MATERIALS, AND BRUSHES

This project uses a whole range of paints—a mixture of flat blue-green vinyl/latex paint, blue and yellow

18-2 A *Design grid—central unicorn panel. Scale the design to suit the size of your selected box. Then trace, reverse, align with the centerline, and repeat.*

powder pigments, and milk for the green-blue ground coat, acrylics and milk paints for the biscuit panels and for the details within the design, straight acrylic paints for the black and red designs and details, and a tinted varnish glaze for the finish. Note that the detail colors are created by mixing the ground and panel colors with the red and black acrylics.

As for brushes, we used just about every brush that we could find—a wide household brush for the ground, a flat, soft-haired watercolor brush for the panels, a good selection of watercolor sables for the details, and a 1″ household brush for the varnish.

MATERIALS

You will need—

• a large chest to decorate
• a sheet each of workout and tracing paper to match the size of your front panel
• a pack of graded sandpapers
• a quantity of instant nonfat dried milk powder
• about ½ pint of silk vinyl/latex paint—we chose a deep blue-green color
• children's powder paint in the colors blue and yellow
• flat acrylic paints in the colors red, biscuit, and black
• a domestic/household paintbrush about 1½″ wide
• a flat watercolor wash brush about 2″ wide
• a good selection of soft-haired, sable watercolor brushes
• a can of clear yacht/spar varnish
• a quantity of mineral/white spirit
• a tube of umber artist's oil-based color paint
• all the usual around-the-house items like newspapers, running water, a pencil and ruler, old cloths, and various old spoons for mixing and stirring

PROJECT STAGES

Preparation
Take your large, found chest, and give it a thorough checking over just to make sure that it's in good sound condition. Of course, we can only assume that you have found a chest that is somewhat like ours—that is, it's in a mess, with dozens of coats of paint and various bits and pieces of hardware screwed and nailed about its surface.

Start by carefully unscrewing the hardware, and making decisions as to whether or not they need to be saved and restored.

Special Tip Our chest had, at some time or other, been covered with fabric material—there were rows of little nails all around the edges. If your chest is in similar condition, don't be tempted to set the nails below the surface; it's much better to spend time carefully easing them out with a pair of pliers.

Once you have removed all of the hardware, fill all of the holes and cracks. When this is done, take a sheet of medium-grade sandpaper, and sand the whole workpiece until the surface is smooth to the touch. Don't bother to remove all of the paint, just make sure that the surface is stable. Having achieved a sound smooth surface, dab areas of bare wood with either varnish or knotting, and let it dry.

Laying On the Ground

Start by running your hands over the whole chest—if it's reasonably smooth and free from splinters and nailheads, then the fun can begin.

Clear the work surface from clutter and set out the milk powder, the blue-green vinyl/latex paint, the green and yellow powder pigment, the biscuit acrylic for the panels, and various spoons, dishes, and containers.

To mix the blue-green ground paint take one cup of milk powder and add cold water until you have a thin syrup. Next, add about one cup of vinyl/latex paint to the milk syrup, and stir them together. Having assessed the color by brushing a few strokes of paint onto a piece of scrap wood and leaving it to dry, then

18-2 B   Design grid—horse and rider side panel. Scale the design to suit the size of your selected box. Then trace and reverse for the two mirror-image side panels.

18-2 C   Design grid—between-panel details. Scale the design to suit the size of your selected box. Then trace and reverse for either side of the centerline.

add small amounts of blue and/or yellow powder pigment to the mix until you have what you consider is a good color.

To mix the biscuit paint for the panels take about ¼ cup of milk powder and add water to make a syrup, then adding small amounts of biscuit acrylic to the syrup until you have a good color.

When you have achieved two vigorous colors, start by painting the whole chest with the blue-green. Let it dry, and then, as needed, lay on another coat to cover.

Draw the three-panel design to fit the size of your chest, and make a clear tracings. Follow the design grid (see **18-2 A** and **B**) for the panel designs and design grids (see **18-2 C** and **D**) for the between-panel

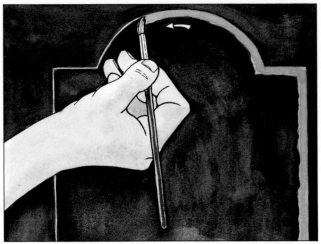

18-3   Use a medium-size brush—work from inside the shape with the point of the brush looking towards the edge. Aim for a positive, flowing line.

18-2 D   Design grid—between-panel design. Scale the design to suit the size of your selected box. Note how the broken line indicates the link-up point between details.

details. When the paint is completely dry, set your chest out with as many guidelines as you think necessary. Then take your tracings, carefully position them on the front of the chest, and fix them in place with tabs of masking tape. Having made absolutely sure that the placing and alignment are correct, use a pencil or a ballpoint pen and a ruler to press-transfer the outline of the three panels.

Remove the tracing paper, and use a soft pencil to rework the transferred lines until they are clearly defined. Take the biscuit color and a fine brush, and very carefully line in the panel shapes (see **18-3**). Finally, take the flat watercolor wash brush, and block in the three panels (see **18-4**). Lay on two or more coats until you have a smooth, dense cover.

Special Tip By ''masking tape'' we mean low-tack drafting tape, as used in design offices. If you use the very sticky tape, then there is a chance that the paint will lift when you remove the tracing paper. If you have doubts, then either hold the tracing paper in place with pins, or with the package-type of lick-and-stick paper tape.

Setting Out the Design

With the chest painted blue-green and the panels painted biscuit, set the tracings back in place on the panels. Press-transfer half the design, reverse the tracing and realign, and then complete the other half (see **18-5**). With the central panel, you just press the design

18-4 *The three panel "windows" painted—ready for the press-transferring. Note the carefully considered proportions and spacing.*

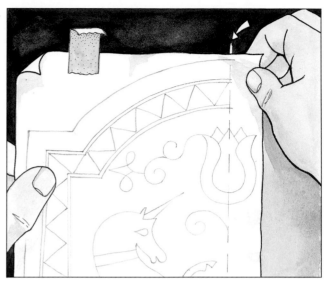

18-5 *Align the half-design with the centerline, then press-transfer, reverse, and repeat.*

through and the job is done. But the easiest technique for the identical, but mirror-image, side panels is to do one panel, and then reverse the same tracing—repeating the procedure for the other panel.

Press-transfer the between-panel details (see **18-2 C** and **D**)—the tulip-vine, the lovebirds, and the hearts—onto the blue ground.

Special Tip It's sometimes difficult to see press-transferred imagery when it has been pressed through to a dark ground—like the dark blue-green color of this chest. If this is the case, you could use a white carbon paper—obtained from specialist art/craft shops.

Finally, remove the tracings, and use a soft pencil and/or a fine-point watercolor felt-tip pen to rework the transferred lines.

Painting the Design

Before you start painting, raise the chest to a comfortable working height, and set out your paint and brushes so that they are close at hand. If you prefer, turn the chest over so that the front panel is uppermost.

Begin by taking the red acrylic paint and a fine-point sable brush and lining in the border lines (see **18-6**). Aim for crisp, clean lines, with the minimum of wobble and deviation.

And so you continue—painting in the red lines of the large stylized flowers at the top-middle of the side panels, the red part of the flower-like motif at the bottom of the panels, and so on.

18-6 *With the drawn design in place, set to work painting the red border lines. Work with a steady, finger-braced dragging stroke. Continue painting in all the red lines that go to make up the design.*

18-7   Mix the red with a small amount of the blue-black ground color to create a harmonious third color. Paint in the triangles in the zigzag border.

Next, take a little of the blue-green ground color, and mix it with the black acrylic until you have a dark blue. Use the color for lining in the zigzag that runs around the inner border (see **18-7**). With the zigzag in place, use the red, dark blue, and a mixture of red and dark blue to block in the triangles. Note how the zigzag triangles run in a color sequence.

Special Tip A foolproof way of ensuring that your detail colors are harmonious is to mix them from your chosen ground colors. For example, if you look at the project picture and other illustrations, you will see that, having restricted our palette to blue-green, biscuit, red, and black, all the other colors are made from combinations of these basic colors. We have mixed the blue-green ground color with black to make a dark blue-black, the blue-black and the red to make a rich purple.

With the red border lines and the zigzags in place, block in all the other large areas of color around the design—the unicorns (see **18-8**), the horses, the horsemen, the vases, the stylized tulips, the love hearts, and so on. First paint the edges of the large areas, and then finish by blocking in.

We have found that the easiest method is to block in several areas in one color and then to move to the other side of the chest and do another color, later returning to the other side of the chest, all the while doing our best to avoid blocks of color that are still wet.

18-8   Since the unicorns are the center of attraction—the pivotal point of the design—do your best to ensure that they are painted with a strong, vigorous stroke.

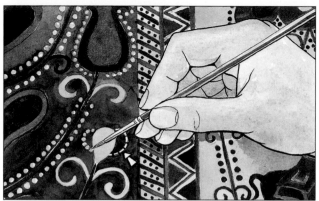

18-9   Dab in the dots with a paint-loaded brush—work around the design, all the while being mindful that the little pools of paint are going to take a long time to dry. Aim for a regular size and spacing of the dots and a smooth natural flow.

When the colors are dry, then comes the good fun bit of painting in the details. Using a fine-point brush, paint in the tendrils on the vines, the wings on the birds, the details of the horsemen, and so on. Take a small brush and the orange-brown paint, and dot in all the little "pearls" that run around the design (see **18-9**).

Special Tip Chests of this character were usually signed and dated—notice how we have put our initials and the date at top center.

Finally, when you figure that you have finished painting, stand well back and give the whole chest a critical once-over. Ask youself, could lines be crisper? are one or two details a bit sloppy? do some colors need a second coat to cover? and so forth.

Finishing
Being happy with the overall design, and when the details are completely dry, clear away all the paints and generally clean up the clutter. This is a good time to wash all the brushes.

Take your finest-grade of sandpaper, and give the whole design a quick sanding. Don't press too hard, just enough to scuff the colors at wear areas and edges. This done, wipe the whole chest with a slightly damp cloth.

Decant about ½ cup of varnish, add a small amount of umber oil color and a dash of mineral/white spirit, and stir to mix. You should finish up with a tinted orange-brown varnish glaze. As needed, add slightly more umber pigment to adjust the color. Give the whole chest one or more coats of varnish glaze, until you have what you consider is a good tint.

Finally, when the varnish is dry, screw on the restored hardware, give the whole chest a wipe-over with wax polish, and the job is done.

AFTERTHOUGHTS

• If you like the project, but are considering using oil-based paints, then be prepared for the long wait between coats. Our chest took about two days to paint—allow at least double that time if you are using oil-based colors.

• If you have to choose between using an old flea market/junk shop chest, and a new one made from something like particleboard, then go for the old solid-wood chest every time.

• If the hardware is in any way interesting, then spend time bringing it to good order. If, for example, the chest has brass handles, be careful that you don't scratch them by using a file or coarse sandpaper—much better, in this case, to use paint stripper, fine-grade steel wool, and metal cleaner.

• If your chest has been given a coat of tar-like varnish, then it's best to have it dipped and stripped professionally.

• Most chests of this character and date were painted and decorated on the top of the lid as well as on all sides. How about it?

• Our found chest had an interesting checker board stencilled on the lid—we decided to leave it be.

—19—
Raspberry Motif Chair

THE PENNSYLVANIA FOLK artists were very fond of decorating small side chairs with painted brush-stroke designs, so much so, that by the second half of the nineteenth century they were producing good numbers of such chairs on a semi-cottage industry basis. This is not to say that they were actually mass-producing the chairs in a factory, only that they were working full-time in small family groups to supply the market.

Although the folk painters used all manner of stylized freehand brush-stroke designs and patterns—everything from birds and flowers to geometrical motifs and abstract blossoms—we consider that perhaps the most beautiful, direct, and spontaneous are the little fruit and vine designs.

19-1   Project picture—the finished chair.

19-2   Design grid—at a scale of four grid squares to 1". (Top) The large splat design. Note the centerline and that the design is not quite symmetrical. (Bottom) The symmetrical small splat design.

It's interesting to note that the designs on these chairs—especially the freehand fruit motifs—were homespun interpretations of painted, bronze stencil designs, as seen on much fancier chairs of the same period. For example, if you look at a gold-on-black Hitchcock-type chair and one or two other mass-produced upmarket chairs that were being made at the time, it's plain to see that the Pennsylvania painters were not above "borrowing" designs. No doubt they came across printed fliers and such, and simply reworked the designs in terms of brush stroke painting.

If you look at our project picture (see **19-1**) and design grid (see **19-2**), you will note that we have drawn inspiration from one of the popular Pennsylvania "arrow-back" side chairs. That is to say, we have copied and modified the characteristic berries, leaves, and tendrils motif for the back splat, the linked hearts for the secondary back splat, and the striping around the leg turnings.

As to our choice of chair, we weren't able to find a suitable arrow-back, but we did come up with a very nice 1920–1930s country chair.

CHOOSING PAINTS, COLORS, MATERIALS, AND BRUSHES

This project uses a flat, pale beige straw-colored vinyl/latex paint for the ground, acrylics for the brush-stroke decoration, and wax varnish followed by wax polish for the finish.

We used a small household brush for the ground and a selection of small and fine-point sable brushes for the details.

MATERIALS

You will need—

• a good-quality country slab-seat-type side chair to decorate, one with horizontal back splats—ours is one of a pair, but it's best if you can get a set of four or six
• a sheet each of workout and tracing paper, to match the size of your chair back splats
• a pack of graded sandpapers
• a quantity of flat vinyl/latex paint, in a pale beige or straw color

131

- flat acrylic paints in the colors red, dark green, and leaf-green
- a domestic/household paintbrush about 1½″ wide
- a selection of soft-haired, sable watercolor brushes—including a fine liner
- a can of clear ''wax'' varnish
- a quantity of mineral/white spirit
- a tin of beeswax furniture polish
- all the usual around-the-house items like newspapers, running water, a pencil and ruler, old cloths, and various old spoons for mixing and stirring

PROJECT STAGES

Preparation

Take you selected chair—ours was covered in thick layers of blue and green paint—and start by turning it upside down and giving it a brief inspection. Examine the underside of the seat for splits, rot, and worm holes, the fit of the legs in the seat, and the fit of the stretcher turnings in the legs. Twist the frame this way and that, and generally see if the chair is sound. Don't worry too much about slightly unsteady, loose legs as long as the seat and back splats are intact. Assuming the chair is in reasonable condition, spend time stripping off the paint.

Having given the chair a swift look-over and removed the paint, then have a good, close look to make sure that the structure is sound. As seems necessary, remove loose legs, scrape off the glue, re-glue, and clamp.

Laying On the Ground

When you are happy with the condition of your selected chair, give it two or more all-over thin coats of flat vinyl/latex paint to cover (see **19-3**).

The order of working is to lay on a coat of paint, let it dry, sand it with the fine-grade sandpaper, lay on another coat, and so on.

Special Tip Don't be tempted to short-cut the painting by laying on great heavy, thick coats of paint. If you do, you will lose most of the turning details and blur the overall image. It's much better to lay on several thin coats, rather than one thick one.

Setting Out the Design

Being mindful that your chair might be of a different design than ours, having only one splat or perhaps three splats, modify the design to fit your selected chair. Draw the motifs to size, and make clear tracings. Note how the large design is not quite symmetrical, and then rework the back of the tracing with a soft pencil.

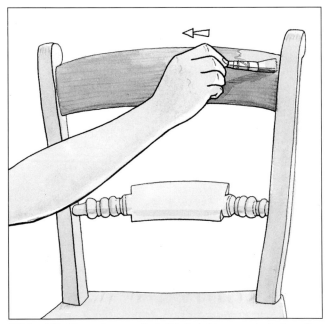

19-3   Working at a comfortable height, start painting the underside, and finish with the back.

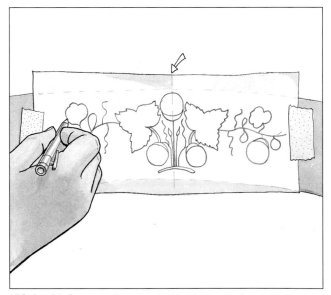

19-4   Make sure that the design is correctly aligned and fixed in place before press-transferring the traced lines.

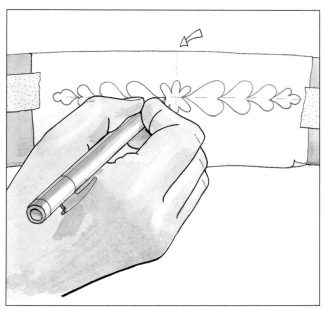

19-5 Align the tracing with the centerline, and carefully press-transfer the lines of the design.

Establish a few pencil guidelines on the splats—a base line and a centerline—align the tracings, and fix them in place with tabs of masking tape (see **19-4**). Use a hard pencil or a ballpoint pen to press-transfer the imagery onto the wood (see **19-5**). Last, remove the tracings, and rework the transferred lines so that the drawn imagery is cleanly established.

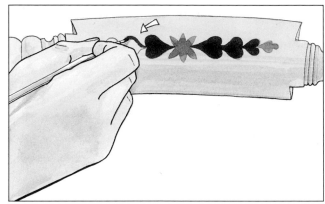

19-7 Use a medium-fine brush to paint the red heart shapes.

Painting the Design

As is the case with any of the projects, by the time you reach the painting stage, the rest is relatively easy. Mix the acrylic paints, select your brushes, and start by blocking all the areas of green (see **19-6**)—the leaves, the cap on the fruits, and the details on the heart motif. There's not much to say about the painting technique other than that we recommend you use a fine brush to establish the limits of the color, and then block in with the larger brush. And the same goes for the red berries and the heart shapes: simply use a fine brush for the color outline (see **19-7**), and then block in with a bigger brush.

19-6 Give the leaves one or more coats of green to cover.

19-8   Use the very fine brush to paint the dark green tendrils, the veins, and the stalks.

Use a fine liner for the dark green details, the tendrils, and the stalks. Keep the strokes lively and dynamic (see **19-8**). Finally, use a small brush and the ground color to dot and dash in the texture on the fruit (see **19-8**, left) and the various rings of color on the leg and splat turnings (see **19-9**, right).

Finishing

When the paints are good and dry, give the whole works a thin coat of wax varnish and allow to dry. Last, give the dry varnish a generous coat of wax polish, and burnish to a deep-shine finish. This last waxing might seem to be a bit of a waste of time, but not at all. The

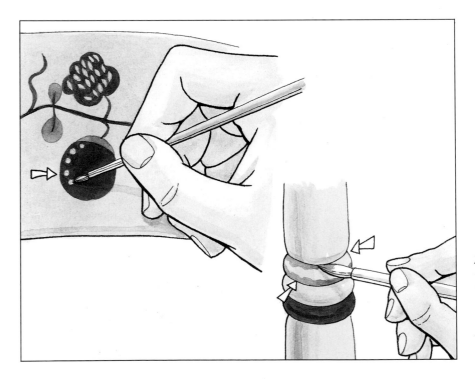

19-9   (Left) Use the fine brush to paint the seeds on the strawberries. Note how there are two kinds of seed shape—long oval dashes in rows and round dots evenly scattered. (Right) Use a medium-fine-point brush to paint into the grooves, and then fill in the remaining areas with a larger brush.

wax not only adds that extra depth to the finish, it also takes away the squeaky friction of the varnish.

AFTERTHOUGHTS

• When you are searching for your chair/s to decorate, it's best to go for the slab-seat type—meaning ones with turned legs and stretchers, and a good width to the horizontal back splat.

• If you decide to use a flat oil-based paint for the ground—rather than a flat vinyl/latex paint—then keep in mind that you will have to wait a day or so for the paint to dry.

• If your found chair has been heavily oiled or waxed, then spend time cleaning it with mineral/white spirit. The best procedure is to clean off the oil/wax with the spirit, and then wash the whole chair with liquid soap.

—20—
Freehand Flower and Leaves on a Hand Mirror

ALTHOUGH THE PENNSYLVANIA folk artists are known primarily for their large, prestigious pieces—the dower chests, wardrobes, dressers, and the like—we must not forget that they also decorated even the most humble workaday items such as buckets, clothes brushes, and spoons. To our way of thinking, there is something rather charming and special about a society that is prepared to spend time decorating items that are not intended for grand display. Somehow or other—and it's not easy to express—we feel a kinship for painters whose primary reward is more in the doing than in the showing off.

When we were searching for a small found item to decorate, we had a real problem; it's amazing how over the last few decades so many of the ordinary small wooden items that we have taken for granted—brushes, brooms, wooden bowls, and such—are either no longer used or have been replaced by items made of plastic.

20-1   Project picture.

Eventually, the best that we could come up with was a small hand mirror (see **20-1**). Okay, so a mirror is a bit more showy than a scrubbing brush, but we feel that its size, shape, and relatively low-key function make it fitting.

CHOOSING PAINTS, COLORS, MATERIALS, AND BRUSHES

This project uses a flat black vinyl/latex paint for the ground, acrylics for the brush-stroke decoration, and wax polish for the finish.

We use a small selection of sable brushes throughout.

MATERIALS

You will need—

• a small wooden item to decorate—a spoon, or brush, or tray, or whatever
• a sheet each of workout and tracing paper, to match the size of your item
• a pack of graded sandpapers
• a quantity of black flat vinyl/latex paint
• flat acrylic paints in the colors dark and light leaf-green, chrome-yellow, red, black, and white
• a selection of soft-haired, sable watercolor brushes—including a fine-point
• a tin of beeswax furniture polish
• all the usual around-the-house items like newspapers, running water, a pencil and ruler, old cloths, and various old spoons for mixing and stirring

PROJECT STAGES

Preparation

As always, take your selected item, and give it a good looking over just to make sure that it's worth decorating. If it's a found item, like our hand mirror, check that it's not actually a valuable object in its own right. If it's new, then make sure that it hasn't in some way been treated with oil or with some virtually irremovable plastic coating.

When you are happy with the piece you have selected, strip off the old paint, and sand the surface with increasingly finer grades of sandpaper. Be very careful not to scour or gouge the wood. And, of course, if your chosen item is coarse-grained, knotty, or whatever, you might also have to apply a wood filler.

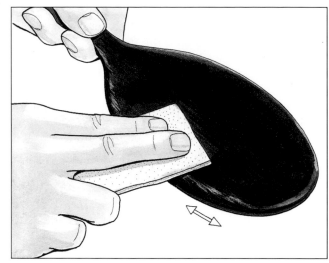

20-2   Sand through the ground to create a "wear" texture.

Depending on the nature of the wood, we tend to remove the worst of the old paint with a knife or scraper, sand down with the medium-grade sandpaper, wipe over with a damp cloth—to raise the grain—and finally rub down with the fine-grade sandpaper until the surface is completely smooth to the touch.

Laying On the Ground
When you have achieved a good, clean, smooth surface, and wiped away the dust, stir the black vinyl/latex paint, choose a suitable-size brush, and lay on a single, thin coat. Wait until the paint is completely dry, give it a quick sanding to remove any raised nibs of grain, and then give it another thin coat to cover.

Special Tip When wood has been brushed/wiped over with water, and allowed to dry, the grain is apt to rise as whiskers and nibs. The painting, sanding, and repainting comprise a technique of gradually achieving a smooth ready-to-decorate surface.

When the paint is completely dry, take the finest grade of sandpaper, and begin the slow, delicate task of cutting through the paint at areas of "wear" (see **20-2**). Don't be tempted to rush, just go at it nice and easy, all the while sanding in the direction of the grain. Stroke away at the edge and curves until little by little you rub through the paint to reveal the color and grain of the underlying wood. It's not such a difficult task, but it can't be rushed.

Setting Out the Design

Having studied our design (see **20-3**) and seen how we have shaped and arranged the motifs to fit the space, draw the imagery to suit the size and shape of your selected item. As needed, add extra leaves or repeat the motifs to fill the space. For example, if you are presented with a circular shape, it might well be fitting that you double up the motifs by mirror-image re-peating so that you have two, more or less identical images set side by side. Trace off the design, and use a soft pencil to rework the lines at the back of the tracing.

Align the tracing within the surface to be decorated, and fix it in place with tabs of masking tape. Use a hard pencil or a ballpoint pen to press-transfer the traced lines onto the wood (see **20-4**).

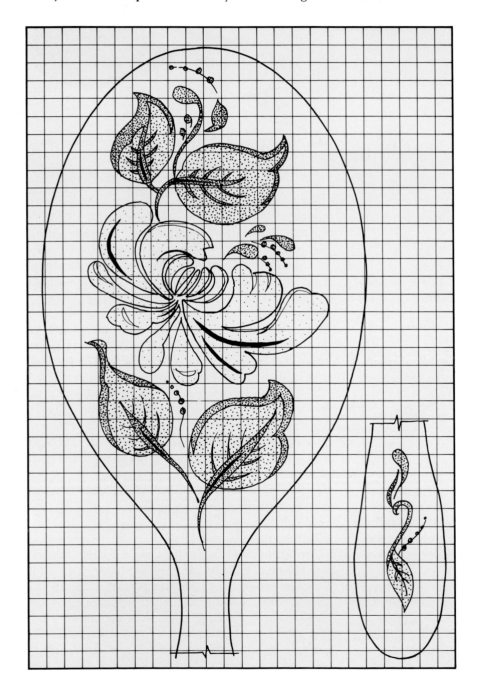

20-3 Design grid—at a scale of four grid squares to 1". For the sake of clarity we haven't shown the black ground.

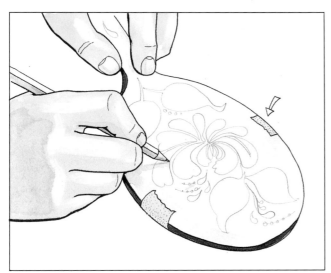

20-4   Only press-transfer the design outlines, and then use those outlines as a guide. You will be able to leave out this stage as you become more confident.

Special Tip If you have to transfer a large, complicated design, then it's best to use a ballpoint pen. Not only does the pen make a clear impression, but, better still, if you use a red ballpoint, for example, then you are better able to see at a glance just how much of the design has been worked.

Finally, remove the tracing and rework the lines so that the shapes and details are clear.

Painting the Design

With imagery positively defined, clear the work surface, and set out your acrylic colors and the brushes. Make sure that the colors are well stirred and of the right consistency.

Starting with the flower at the middle of the design, the order of work is to load your brush with chrome-yellow, wipe the head to a point, set it down at the center of the flower, and run the brush out in a single sweep to make the petal-shaped stroke of color (see **20-5**, top left). And, of course, if you are working a large petal with a small brush, you might have to run another stroke to the side of the first to complete the shape. And so you continue with the flower, loading the brush with color, wiping the head of the brush to a point, setting the paint down at the middle of the flower, and then completing the stroke with a positive, down-on-and-off flourish. Work around the flower so that all the strokes are easy and smoothly curved. Use

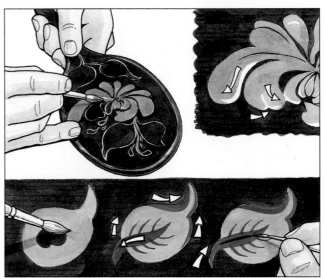

20-5   (Top left) To paint the yellow flower, use the medium-large sable brush with confident sweeping strokes. (Top right) Paint the white highlights with the fine brush—aim for swift, delicate dashes of white. (Bottom, left to right) Paint the entire leaf shape light green. Overpaint with dark green for the vein and edge details. Finally, use the very fine brush to paint the black crease lines in the middle.

the fine brush to paint the dashes of white highlight on the petals (see **20-5**, top right).

To paint the leaves, take a brush and the light green color, and block in the shape of each leaf with as few strokes as possible (see **20-5**, bottom left). Follow through with the dark green details. If you have a look at the drawings, you will see that you can just about complete a leaf shape with ten strokes of dark green (see **20-5**, middle bottom). Make a stroke at each side to define the pointed shape, a single stroke at the center for the middle vein and the stalk, and then a few swift little strokes at either side of the stalk for the secondary veins. Finish the leaves by painting the black middle vein dashes with the fine-point brush (see **20-5**, bottom right).

Special Tip If you are a beginner, and bearing in mind that to a great extent the success of this project hinges on the flowers and leaves being swiftly painted with the minimum of strokes, then it might be wise to spend time practising your brush strokes. Half the secret is having good brushes and knowing what sort of stroke such and such a brush is likely to produce.

20-6   Use the fine brush to paint the red tendrils and berries/buds.

With the flowers and leaves in place, use the fine-point brush to line-in the little red dashes and the little dots of red that suggest trails of berries or buds (see **20-6**).

Finishing

When you are pleased with the painted imagery and have waited for the paint to dry, take the fine-grade sandpaper and gently stroke the surface to ever so slightly cut through the paint (see **20-7**). Once again, don't be in a hurry to get the job done, just go at it nice and easy—with a soft, caressing touch.

Finally, give the whole works a generous coat of beeswax polish, and burnish it to a deep-shine finish (see **20-8**).

20-7   Use a threefold pad of fine-grade sandpaper to give the face of the work a quick, light sanding.

20-8   Use a pad of soft cloth to wax and burnish—work the polish well into the texture of the paint.

AFTERTHOUGHTS

• When you are searching for an item to decorate, it's best to go for a small workaday item, like a clothes brush, a spoon, or a kitchen cutting board.

• Since this project is all about creating flowers and leaves with single, swift brush strokes, the images must stay more or less the same size. The item to be decorated either needs to be small, or you have to increase the number of motifs.

Metric Conversion

Inches to Millimetres and Centimetres						
MM—*millimetres* CM—*centimetres*						
Inches	**MM**	**CM**	**Inches**	**CM**	**Inches**	**CM**
⅛	3	0.3	9	22.9	30	76.2
¼	6	0.6	10	25.4	31	78.7
⅜	10	1.0	11	27.9	32	81.3
½	13	1.3	12	30.5	33	83.8
⅝	16	1.6	13	33.0	34	86.4
¾	19	1.9	14	35.6	35	88.9
⅞	22	2.2	15	38.1	36	91.4
1	25	2.5	16	40.6	37	94.0
1¼	32	3.2	17	43.2	38	96.5
1½	38	3.8	18	45.7	39	99.1
1¾	44	4.4	19	48.3	40	101.6
2	51	5.1	20	50.8	41	104.1
2½	64	6.4	21	53.3	42	106.7
3	76	7.6	22	55.9	43	109.2
3½	89	8.9	23	58.4	44	111.8
4	102	10.2	24	61.0	45	114.3
4½	114	11.4	25	63.5	46	116.8
5	127	12.7	26	66.0	47	119.4
6	152	15.2	27	68.6	48	121.9
7	178	17.8	28	71.1	49	124.5
8	203	20.3	29	73.7	50	127.0

1 liter	= 0.42 cups
1 cup	= 0.24 liters

Index

143

About the Authors

ALAN AND GILL (for Gillian) Bridgewater, a unique husband-and-wife team, have gained an international reputation as producers of crafts books of the highest calibre. Concentrating on woodwork, woodcarving, and folk art, they are regarded internationally as authorities on Pacific Northwest Native American totems and masks, toys, chip carving, misericords, carved and painted furniture, and nautical carving. The perfect partnership: Gill does all the step-by-step illustrations, Alan does the technical illustrations and writes the text, and they both roll up their sleeves for the hands-on crafts.

The Bridgewaters met at art school, they have two sons, and they live in Cornwall, England.

They have produced more than thirty books to date, including this and the following titles published by STERLING PUBLISHING COMPANY:

- Carving Figureheads & Other Nautical Designs
- Carving Totem Poles & Masks
- Folk Art Woodcarving: 823 Detailed Patterns
- Making Noah's Ark Toys in Wood
- Power Tool Woodcarving
- Traditional Pull-Along Toys in Wood
- Treasury of Woodcarving Designs
- Woodturning Traditional Folk Toys